"Whether you're writing a comedy or a drama, a feature or a pilot, Klick's book is an invaluable resource, a hand-holding guide to infusing every moment of your story with something so important it's almost always overlooked or misused: the element of surprise."
— Chad Gervich, writer/producer: *After Lately*, *Cupcake Wars*, *Wipeout*; author: *Small Screen, Big Picture: A Writer's Guide to the TV Business*

"A minute-by-minute, beat-by-beat way at looking at story and structure. If you've ever heard that writing a screenplay is like putting together a puzzle, here are all the pieces you need. Klick's use of using examples from dozens of films creates a fantastic guide to improving your script."
— Matthew Terry, filmmaker/screenwriter/teacher, columnist for HollywoodLitSales.com

"In *Something Startling Happens*, Todd Klick demystifies how to approach the scriptwriting process and takes you on a beautiful journey into the thought process behind the moments that make a feature great. Since Todd is coming from the screenwriter/executive perspective, he did the work of analysis and you get to reap the rewards of what he found. He will give you tons of *aha!* thoughts and will help you to look at and interpret story in a way that will give you answers on how to best write your script."
— Jen Grisanti, author of *Story Line: Finding Gold In Your Life Story*, writing instructor for Writers on the Verge with NBC, blogger for The Huffington Post

"When I sit down with screenwriting students, one of the most useful exercises is to 'beat' out the story with them. Todd Klick's *Something Startling Happens* is a catalyst for developing compelling and engaging screenplays. It is a new and unique tool in the storytelling process."
— Rob Goald, UNLV Film Dept.

"Having sold over 100 scripts and written for virtually every network and studio, I learned early on how vital structure was to crafting a successful script. I tell the writers I mentor to study movies and break down their structure — Todd Klick has done this for them, minute by minute, via numerous hit films over a variety of genres. This book can be an invaluable tool in building a professional career."

> — Marc Scott Zicree, writer: *The Twilight Zone Companion, Star Trek: The Next Generation, Deep Space Nine, Babylon 5*

"Finally, a refreshing new approach to an old art. Todd Klick has not only written the consummate go-to guide for writing better screenplays, but his book also unveils the timeless page-by-page structure that pro screenwriters instinctively, if not secretly, use. This book will help propel your scripts — old and new — to professional heights."

> — Kevin Bernhardt, screenwriter: *The Peaceful Warrior, Elephant White*

"A dazzling new nuts-a-bolts story guide that reveals the extremely important 'in betweens' left out in other screenwriting books. The perfect companion to Blake Snyder's *Save The Cat!*."

> — John Philip Dayton, executive producer, producer, director, writer: *The Waltons, Eight Is Enough, The New Adventures of Wonder Woman, Matlock*

SOMETHING STARTLING HAPPENS

The 120 Story Beats
Every Writer Needs To Know

TODD KLICK

Published by Michael Wiese Productions
12400 Ventura Blvd. #1111
Studio City, CA 91604
tel. 818.379.8799
fax 818.986.3408
mw@mwp.com
www.mwp.com

Cover design: Johnny Ink www.johnnyink.com
Book design: Gina Mansfield Design

Printed by McNaughton & Gunn, Inc., Saline, Michigan
Manufactured in the United States of America

Library of Congress Cataloging-in-Publication Data

Klick, Todd, 1976-
Something startling happens : the 120 story beats every writer
needs to know : a minute-by-minute guide for all screenwriters, directors, producers, actors, editors, graphic novelists,
development execs, and cinematic novelists / Todd Klick.
       p. cm.
 Includes filmography.
 ISBN 978-1-61593-059-3
1. Motion picture authorship--Handbooks, manuals, etc. I.
Title.
 PN1996.K62 2011
 808'.066791--dc22

                                        2011017648

The author acknowledges the copyright owners of the following motion pictures from which references and single frames have been used in this book for purposes of commentary, criticism and scholarship under the Fair Use Doctrine.

....

About A Boy © 2002 Universal, All Rights Reserved.

Alien © 1979 Twentieth Century-Fox, All Rights Reserved.

All The President's Men © 1976 Warner Bros., All Rights Reserved.

Amélie © 2001 ZOE, All Rights Reserved.

Being John Malkovich © 1999 Universal, All Rights Reserved.

Braveheart © 1992 Paramount, All Rights Reserved.

Casablanca © 1942 Warner Bros., All Rights Reserved.

Die Hard © 1988 Twentieth Century-Fox, All Rights Reserved.

Erin Brockovich © 2000 Universal, All Rights Reserved.

Fight Club © 1999 Twentieth Century-Fox, All Rights Reserved.

Forrest Gump © 1994 Paramount, All Rights Reserved.

The Game © 1997 PolyGram, All Rights Reserved.

The Godfather © 1992 Paramount, All Rights Reserved.

Ghost © 1990 Paramount, All Rights Reserved.

Halloween © 1978 Compass International, All Rights Reserved.

Hannah and Her Sisters ©1986 Orion, All Rights Reserved.

Jaws ©1975 Universal, All Rights Reserved.

Juno © 2007 Fox Searchlight, All Rights Reserved.

Kill Bill © 2003 Miramax, All Rights Reserved.

Knocked Up © 2007 Universal, All Rights Reserved.

Little Miss Sunshine © 2006 Fox Searchlight, All Rights Reserved.

DEDICATION

To the maestros who taught me story
through their extraordinary work:

Ray Bradbury, Richard Matheson,
Stephen King, John Steinbeck,
Michael Crichton, Rod Serling,
John Irving, Woody Allen,
J.D. Salinger, Steven Spielberg,
George Lucas, Martin Scorsese,
Ron Howard, David Mamet,
Spalding Gray, Robert Towne,
William Goldman, Frank Miller,
Cameron Crowe, Guillermo Del Toro,
James Cameron, Christopher Nolan,
Bryan Singer, Paul Schrader,
Robert Benton, Billy Wilder,
Zack Snyder, Danny Boyle,
Terry Gilliam, Clint Eastwood,
David Fincher, Francis Ford Coppola,
Wes Anderson, David Lynch,
Paul Thomas Anderson, Steven Soderbergh,
Oliver Stone, Edward Robb Ellis,
Blake Snyder, Kevin Smith,
Quentin Tarantino, Andrew Kevin Walker,
Alfred Hitchcock, Nick Hornby,
Philip Roth, Spike Lee,
Richard Linklater, Ridley Scott,
Gus Van Sant, Shane Black, David Koepp,
Aaron Sorkin, M. Night Shyamalan,
Charlie Kaufman, Joel & Ethan Coen, J.J. Abrams,
Sam Raimi, Alvin Sargent, John Hughes,
Tony Gilroy, David Chase, John Milius.

TABLE OF CONTENTS

PREFACE

This book's purpose is to expose and explore the 120 minute-by-minute story beats that unite all successful films. In other words, this book reveals what all great movies do exactly the same during each and every minute, no matter what genre, decade it was made, or nationality of the filmmaker. I hope that the insights unearthed within these pages will give screenwriters, directors, producers, actors, development execs, managers, agents, editors, graphic novelists, and traditional novelists who wish to write more cinematically, the same consecutive page-by-page beats that all influential films utilize.

To prove my theory under rigorous conditions, I chose films made over a 60-year time span. I also picked writer/directors who possess wildly different styles to demonstrate that the minute-by-minute beats universally apply. My goal was to put filmmakers as diverse as Steven Spielberg, Woody Allen, Sam Raimi, The Wachowski Brothers, George Lucas, John Carpenter, Robert Zemeckis, Jason Reitman, Francis Ford Coppola, Akira Kurosawa, Tony Scott, John McTiernan, Wes Craven, Judd Apatow, Spike Jonze, Sydney Pollock, Jonathan Dayton & Valerie Faris, M. Night Shyamalan, and Quentin Tarantino side-by-side to confirm that supposed highbrow auteurs abide by the same minute-by-minute story rules as independent filmmakers and hip guns-and-guts writer/directors.

The movies that were selected for this book have garnered critical or financial success. Of the 43 movies used as examples, most have been "Certified Fresh" by the popular movie review website Rotten Tomatoes (*rottentomatoes.com*). On the site, movies with a "Tomatometer" of 75% or better, and feature at least 40 reviews from critics (including five "Top Critics"), receive the "Certified Fresh" seal. Most of the movies in this book are in the 80%–100% range, either with the critics or audiences.

As far as terminology, my goal was simple: Develop short phrases that encapsulated the core of each movie minute's commonality. For example, if something jaw dropping happens during a particular minute in every good movie, I called it the "Jaw Dropper."

Speaking of Jaw Droppers, there were many people whose kindnesses made my jaw drop during the writing of this book. Special thanks to Ann Stewart for editing my manuscript in its early stages, and to Michael Bacall for photographing a few movie stills for me in a time of need. Deep appreciation to Gil Fortis for allowing me access to his high-quality DVD collection, and to Blake Snyder for his advice and encouragement — you are missed. Thank you as well to Merrill Capps, who took the author photo; John Dayton; Alan Denman; Ayesha Walker; my mom, Betty; my dad, Merlin; my sister, Wendy; Jay Klick; Craig and Heather Donmoyer; Eric Bierker; Zach Lewis, Rob Flieschman; Gerald Collins; and Ken Lee and Michael Wiese.

Todd Klick
Santa Monica, CA
writerwrench.com

THE STORY

I remember exactly when the thunderbolt for this book struck me.

I was living in Gettysburg, Pennsylvania, in a rented country home close to where the first shots of the famous Civil War battle were fired. I had moved there during the later part of an intensive writing odyssey that took me through France, Italy, Mexico's Mayan ruins, and finally to this historic battlefield where General Lee once led his Confederate troops on horseback, and Abraham Lincoln delivered his Address for the ages. I had quit the corporate advertising world a year earlier to pursue the study of storytelling. Keeping up the grueling long hours of advertising at that time while simultaneously pursuing creative writing was wearing me thin. To fit in more writing practice, I would secretly type my plays and screenplays in a tiny text box on my work screen's lower right hand corner, and then write for hours more in the evenings and weekends. I was able to win a few short story contests with my limited time, and co-write a successful play about Milton Hershey — the founder of Hershey's Chocolate — that packed theaters for three years in the Pennsylvania heartland where I was raised. But I knew there were volumes more to learn about the craft of storytelling, and the corporate life was slowing me down from gaining that knowledge.

Over the years the advertising agency grew, and more work piled onto my desk to "increase productivity." As a result, my already tiny writing box shrunk smaller and smaller. Before the box vanished completely, I did the unthinkable in the eyes of my coworkers: I quit my job, burned my work ID badge with lighter fluid — the same ID we were forced to wear around our necks like dog leashes — sold my house, cashed out my 401(k), and moved to Europe to flee the ringing phone and focus on writing full time. While there, I wrote faithfully from

8 a.m.–3 p.m. every day, figuring out the inner workings of story, especially movie stories which moved me to tears quicker than any other art form. During this time I re-studied all the writing and screenwriting books I had previously dog-eared and underlined to tatters. I also filled reams of yellow legal pads as I broke down more than 300 movies, writing in great detail what the filmmakers intended with each scene, and how the scenes fit into the whole.

That's what I was doing on that humid August night in Gettysburg when it all started coming together. I was analyzing *Raiders of the Lost Ark* scene by scene. The aroma of a nearby apple orchard wafted in through the screen windows as I scribbled notes on the opening sequence where Indiana Jones stands before the golden idol inside the forbidden temple. Stroking his chin, Indy fills a bag with sand, trying to guess the weight of the coveted booty. Doing a quick swap with the gold artifact, he holds the idol, elated. Suddenly, the idol's pedestal sinks and the ceiling crumbles, startling the hell out of Indy. As soon as this exciting moment started, I hit pause on my DVD player and re-checked my notes. Something odd was going on during Minute 8, but I wasn't sure quite what. I then re-examined my notes for *The Matrix*. During Minute 8 Neo sits alone in his apartment, emailing back and forth with Trinity. Trinity closes the conversation with the words: "Knock Knock, Neo." Just then, two hard knocks on the door *startle* Neo.

That was twice something startling happened during that particular minute.

I rifled through my stack of notebooks, searching for what happens during Minute 8 in other movies. What I found astonished me: In *The Sixth Sense*, a half-naked man *startles* Malcolm by pointing a gun at him. In *Tootsie*, Michael's friends *startle* him with a surprise birthday party. In *Jaws*, the gruesome state of the shark-eaten girl *startles* Chief

Brody. In *Halloween*, an escaped mental patient leaps onto the car and *startles* the nurse. In *Scream*, the disturbed caller *startles* Casey by gutting her boyfriend. Over and over this Minute 8 "startling" phenomenon appeared, no matter what genre I chose. *Does this happen even in a Charlie Kaufman movie?* I wondered. All my writing friends told me that Kaufman broke all the screenwriting rules. Inserting *Being John Malkovich* into my DVD player, I queued my stopwatch and pressed play. As the movie entered Minute 8 I leaned forward, wondering if something startling would happen here too. In that scene, John Cusack's character, Craig, takes a rather boring elevator ride toward his job interview. Suddenly, the woman riding with him presses the stop button. The elevator jerks to an ugly halt and an ear-piercing alarm *startles* Craig! I about fell off my couch. This was a story insight that every screenwriting book failed to mention. As a result, I spent the entire sleepless night popping in all the movies in my extensive collection, including foreign and independent films, rigorously testing this Minute 8 theory. Startling moment after moment kept happening, without exception. Since each script page represents a minute of screen time, I now knew that something startling *had* to happen on Page 8 in my screenplays. Why hadn't anyone written about this? This information could be tremendously helpful to screenwriters.

The next evening, I delved deeper into movies and my notes, breaking them down *minute by minute* instead of the traditional scene by scene. What I discovered raised goose bumps on my arms, and continues to do so to this day. Good movies do the *exact* same things, across the board, in succession, during each and every minute. Doesn't matter if it's Minute 1 or 101. Even if one movie ends at Minute 85 and the next ends at 120, they still abide by this strict minute-by-minute blueprint.

This was an unbelievable revelation — one that made total sense once I understood why. On average, movies only have 90 to 120 minutes to tell a complete, satisfying story. That's hardly any time compared to the breadth of a novel. The singer-songwriter, Sting, once said that rock-and-roll has to "burn from the first bar," meaning that the song has to hit the ground running and not let up until it's finished. So do films. Every minute in a movie *must* count. [Every minute *has* to satisfy a specific story function.] If it doesn't adhere to this minute-by-minute rhythm, the audience feels it. It's a deep psychological structure that's been honed for more than a century by audiences and film-makers. All great writers, directors, and editors seem to have this innate minute-by-minute rhythm, or eventually find the rhythm through thousands of hours of hard work and study.

It's like this: Good films go through an extensive distilling process that eventually forces the movie to fall into step with this universal, minute-to-minute cadence. The process starts with the screenwriter who bangs his or her head for weeks, months, or even years, figuring out the initial story; then the directors and actors add more insights as they film the pages; then the editor whittles and tightens the story even further. More shaping and additions occur after executives' notes and test screenings. The entire process chips away the unnecessary and adds the necessary until it becomes the classic we all know and love today.

If I dare say, this book has captured that rhythm. This is the guide I've been searching the shelves for my entire writing life, and I'd like to share it with you. I did the legwork so you don't have to. Using a stopwatch, I took meticulous notes while analyzing hundreds of movies during a three-year period. I took the job seriously because I take writing and movies seriously. At times I had three films screening simultaneously: One movie on a laptop, another on a bigger TV, and yet another on a flip-open DVD player. When you study films side-by-side like this, the minute-by-minute commonalities become glaringly, and excitingly, obvious. Another benefit of this book is that it walks you through each script page's beat instead of avoiding the vast — but crucially important — chasms between major plot points ignored by all other resources. This book shows you the desperately needed "in betweens." As soon as I started applying these minute-by-minute beats to my newest scripts, as if by magic I attracted my first manager, made the prestigious Nicholl Fellowship quarterfinals, the PAGE International Screenplay finals, received four options, signed a deal with the Hallmark Channel, and became a Director of Story Development in Los Angeles. What you will learn in this book works if applied with passion and commitment. Flip through the pages and you'll immediately experience the same "Aha!" moments I was having. I promise.

Let the thunderbolts begin!

HOW TO USE THIS BOOK

The best way to use *Something Startling Happens* depends on what type of writer you are. Are you a Stephen King type, or a John Irving type? King said his writing process is *"like walking through a desert and all at once, poking up through the hardpan, I see the top of a chimney. I know there's a house down there, and I'm pretty sure that I can dig it up if I want."* Without a complete idea of where his story is headed, King starts writing the book, making the discoveries as he plows forward. John Irving, on the other hand, outlines extensively, knowing the fine details of each scene and chapter before he even begins writing his novel.

Whether you are a King or an Irving type of writer, or you approach story from a completely different place altogether, you can use *Something Startling Happens* as a page-by-page metaphor or checklist whenever you're ready for it, or as an idea booster if you get stuck. If you're an Irving type of writer, you may want to do your research first, develop your extensive outline, write your first draft, then reference this book to see if you're addressing each minute-by-minute guideline. Or maybe you want to find your story on your own, and write a voluminous 300-page first draft to get it all out of your head. Cool, go do it. That's fantastic. But eventually you may want to visit this book to see if your script addresses the successful minute-by-minute beats. Whatever type of writer you are, this book is here to help during any stage of your personal process.

When in need, this book can assist in filling in weak spots while developing your overall outline or treatment structure. Or you can use it to brainstorm with other writers on how your story should advance or conclude, or to think up fresh ways to surprise the audience that is consistent with the minute beats and genre.

When it comes to my own process, I hone a 17-page outline until the story is structurally sound, then when I write the script I reference the *Something Startling Happens* beats as I enter each page. When I first applied the minute-by-minute beats (as mentioned earlier), *that's* when I attracted my first manager and advanced quickly to the Nicholl Fellowship quarters. Soon after, I had to hustle to meet another contest deadline with a new script. I didn't have two months to outline like I usually did, so I decided to jump right in and "bang it out blind." Starting at page one with only a grabber opening in mind, I wrote like Stephen King — discovering the story as I went along. As I approached each script page, I referenced *Something Startling Happens* to keep me on track so I didn't waste time. I wrote the script in two weeks (a personal record), and sent it off immediately to the PAGE International Screenwriting Awards, where I eventually made the finals. My latest script using *Something Startling Happens* as my guide has recently attracted A-list creative talent who have worked on such blockbuster movies as *Spider-Man*, *Wall-E*, *Forrest Gump*, and *Up In The Air*. I owe this attention to the minute-by-minute insights revealed in this book.

Something Startling Happens is not limited only to writers and novelists who desire to write more cinematically. Directors, producers, actors, and editors may also find this book beneficial as a production checklist. Are you, as a director, producer or editor, hitting these minute-to-minute beats while you're filming and editing? If not, you may be in for expensive re-shoots to eventually capture these moments after test screenings.

FIVE THINGS YOU NEED TO KNOW BEFORE YOU BEGIN

1) I want to make something clear: The minute-by-minute beats you are about to read are *not* taken from the original screenplays or shooting scripts. They are drawn from far superior material: The final stories you see on the big screen *after* they were filtered through the studio distilling process.

2) You need to understand that the terms used in this book (like *Hero*, *Ally*, *Bad Guy*, *Enemy*) are flexible and interchangeable from page to page.

Sometimes the enemy becomes the hero for a page (in *Spider-Man*, Osborn becomes the hero when the evil board members want to sell his company); or the ally becomes the enemy (in *Top Gun*, Commander Metcalf becomes Maverick's enemy in the training session); or the hero can become the bad guy (Peter argues with Uncle Ben, who is only trying to help him).

Sometimes the ally can be an inanimate object (in *The Sixth Sense*, the cassette player becomes Malcolm's ally, revealing information he needs to know), or the hero's conscience can become the bad guy (in *Spider-Man*, Peter's conscience becomes his enemy). You must be flexible with these terms or the beats won't work for you.

I also use words like *explosion*, *damage*, *warning*, or *threat*. Most times an "explosion" will be a literal explosion, or the explosion could be more figurative, like an *explosion of emotion*. A warning can sometimes be very dramatic, or inconspicuous. The dramatic level of these words can change from page to page, or story to story. But what's important to realize is that they are there. These beats should be represented on every page, grand or small, or your screenplay may fall short. The

xxii **SOMETHING STARTLING HAPPENS** | todd klick

reader or audience expects these patterns subconsciously. If you neglect to include them, they may feel gypped.

3) You need to use the minute-by-minute catch phrases. I spent months paring down the phrases so they are descriptive and precise. The phrases were initially one sentence long, but after using them while wrestling with my own scripts, I found myself paraphrasing: "This is Minute 63, I need an *Ally Attack*." Or, "This is Minute 77, I gotta have *The Rumble*." These fun phrases get to the point of what needs to happen in the script — a tremendous timesaver. Writing partners and I use the catch phrases as shorthand. We even use the phrases while developing stories with clients, with other screenwriters, and during pitch meetings. The phrases work for us, and they'll work for you too.

4) If you're fond of using index cards while developing your story, this is a technique you'll find helpful. After you've outlined your movie, scribble the minute-by-minute catch phrases onto 120 individual index cards, each card representing one minute. Then write down on the card original ways you can demonstrate that minute in your story. For example, write as many *Friend Or Fist* moments you can think of on Card 6 (Minute 6), or write as many *Whew, That Was Close!* moments as you can on Card 15 (Minute 15). This will help you to focus your creativity and force originality.

5) You must put in the hard work. The beats are laid out nicely for you in this book, but you still must roll up your sleeves and write and rewrite obsessively. In other words, precision white lines are painted onto the tennis court, and the net is raised to the official 36 inches, but the player must still step within those rigidly structured lines and exert the tremendous physical effort required to finish the match. And if the player expects to win, he must play the match with creative ground strokes and effective net play.

You must do the same with your story.

HOW TO BREAK DOWN MOVIES ON YOUR OWN

"How do I break down movies minute-by-minute for myself?" you may ask. It's easy, and I'll walk you through a few exercises in this book to help you get the hang of it. But if you want to start now, rent the movie you want to analyze. I recommend Netflix because of their immense catalog, much of which you can stream instantly online. Or Redbox for newer movies. Grab a stopwatch and click it on until it reaches 1:00 (one minute). Why 1:00? Starting your stopwatch at 1:00 instead of 0:00 will create less confusion with your analysis, believe me. It's simply easier for 1:00 to equal Page 1 of your screenplay than for 0:00 to equal Page 1. Starting at 1:00 means that 1:00 = the top of Page 1, 2:00 = the top of Page 2 and 3:00 = the top of Page 3, etc. When you use 1:00 as your starting point while studying any movie, you'll know instantly, for example, that when your stopwatch reaches 5:30 that you're halfway through your screenplay's Page 5, or that 53:45 means that you're three-quarters of the way through your script's Page 53.

Okay, begin the movie. Now, *when* you restart your stopwatch is crucial. Don't click on your stopwatch as soon as the credits begin. Start when the *story* begins. How do you know when the story begins? It's where the screenwriter most likely began writing the movie after typing FADE IN. Don't start when the credits are running, unless the credits are shown while the story is unfolding (as in *Raiders of the Lost Ark*). And also be on the lookout for what I call "James Bond credits," meaning: Credits that appear after the big movie opening. Click your stopwatch off during the James Bond credits and music, unless of course they're part of the story. Use this book as a guide as you stop and start each minute, jotting down your own insights.

NOTE: This is an advanced screenwriting book. Before you begin it, I'd recommend that you know story basics first, like character arc, theme, sequences, Inciting Incidents, beats, etc. You need to understand these foundational elements before you start writing to these minute-by-minute rhythms. If you lack storytelling basics, you'll get frustrated pretty quickly while writing. I highly recommend Lajos Egri's *The Art of Dramatic Writing*, *Save The Cat!* by Blake Snyder, *Essentials of Screenwriting* by Richard Walter, and *Aristotle's Poetics for Screenwriters* by Michael Tierno. These books will get you quickly up to speed.

FREQUENTLY ASKED QUESTIONS

"What happens if a film is only 85 minutes long? Do the beats you describe get compressed — sometimes two per page?"

Whether the story stops at Minute 86 (like *Halloween*) or 120 (like *Jaws*), the minute-by-minute (page-by-page) beats remain steadfastly consistent. *Halloween* and *Jaws* do the exact same minute-by-minute beats up until Minute 86. *Halloween* ends there. *Jaws* continues, adhering to the remaining minute-by-minute beats. Therefore, compressing story beats is unnecessary.

"If every good movie sticks to these minute-by-minute beats, then why are some movies longer than others?"

Movie lengths vary for this reason: The number and complexity of characters and subplots change from film to film, requiring different lengths to satisfy each unique story arc. But whether the film has a handful of subplots, or just one, the writer must still address each minute-by-minute benchmark mentioned in this book if they wish to avoid boring the audience — an audience, by the way, who inherently expects this underlying story rhythm in all the movies they watch.

"Sometimes movies are more than 120 minutes long. Do the minute-by-minute beats extend beyond the two hours mentioned in your book?"

Yes, I originally wrote this book to address movies up to 3 hours long, but since the majority of movies sold and distributed are under 120 minutes, I decided to trim the book to accommodate the practical needs of the average working screenwriter and filmmaker.

Do these beats work with different genres?

Yes, which I will demonstrate by using five different genres in a case study throughout this book. What's great about these beats is that it doesn't matter if you're writing a thriller, a romantic comedy, horror, drama, action adventure, or a combination of two or three genres, the underlining minute-by-minute beats are still represented in all successful movies. It's the ground floor of what all movie stories are built upon.

Is this a formula way of storytelling? Won't a formula stifle my creativity?

The definition of "formula" is: *"A conventionalized statement expressing some fundamental principle."* Is *Something Startling Happens* a fundamental principle? Absolutely *yes*. It's a universal principle that is common in all successful movie stories. You're welcome to avoid these fundamental principles in your storytelling, but don't be surprised if agents, managers, studio execs, or production companies don't return your phone calls or emails after you send them your script or independent movie. In addition to looking for a fresh voice in your work, they are subconsciously looking for these universal beats when they're reading your screenplay or viewing your film — it's a primal need fashioned over a hundred years of industry storytelling. If you're an experimental independent filmmaker who is fiercely against anything that whiffs of a set way of doing things, fine, go do your thing. But don't be shocked when your audience falls asleep during your screenings, or walks out altogether. There's a reason why fundamental principles, like geometry or physics, keep a plane in the air, or prevent a skyscraper from toppling over: They work! So it is with the fundamentals of storytelling. Will these fundamental principles stifle your creativity? Quite the opposite! Once you know the fundamental beats, it frees you to spend your creative time thinking of original ways of telling your story each and every minute! For example, once Picasso mastered the fundamental principles of color and design, it freed him to go in a completely different direction visually than all the other painters who preceded him. But here's the thing: Even though Picasso's cubist creations looked radically different than anything else the gallery audiences had seen up until that point, each of Pablo's successful paintings, at their core, still adhered to the basic fundamental principles of color and design. Once he mastered the universal basics and applied them, it freed him to spend all of his energy creating original, timeless pieces! So it can be with your stories!

Will these beats work for short films?

Whether your short film is 5 minutes long, 20 minutes long, or 45 minutes long, the minute-by-minute beats apply. You still must satisfy Socrates' theory that all stories need a beginning, middle, and end, but underneath the beginning-middle-end, no matter what your story's length, the *Something Startling Happens* beats remain a universal rhythm for any visual storytelling length.

Can I use these beats when writing television pilots?

Yes, the minute-by-minute beats work whether you're writing a 22-minute comedy pilot, an hour-long crime drama, or a two-hour TV movie. *Something Startling Happens'* universal story rhythms apply whether you're watching a blockbuster on a giant Cineplex screen, or a popular series on a tiny home television. All visual stories still need Minute 5's *Jaw Dropper*, Minute 14's *Danger Watch*, or Minute 22's *Truth Declared*, etc.

How about a webisode? Do the Something Startling Happens *patterns work for those?*

Yes, whether your webisode is 3 minutes long or up to 10 minutes long, the opening minute-by-minute beats need to be applied — along with Socrates' beginning-middle-end storytelling theory — to satisfy the audience's inherent rhythms and expectations. During Minutes 1 through 10 the audience will need to experience *Attension, The Build, The Ratchet, Another Notch, Jaw Dropper, Friend Or Fist, Friend Or Fist 2, Something Startling Happens, The Pursuit, The Discussion,* etc.

How can a director use Something Startling Happens*?*

A director can use the minute-by-minute beats in this book as a checklist while working with a writer, developing storyboards with an artist, or on-set while working with the director of photography. A director can also use the phrases in this book as verbal shorthand when discussing a story with a producer, actor, or DP.

How can a producer use Something Startling Happens*?*

If a producer finds a script he likes, but feels there's something missing in its storytelling, the producer can use *Something Startling Happens* to diagnose what's missing. The producer can also refer to this book while working with a director to assure that his movie is hitting all the same rhythms that all successful movies are utilizing.

How can an editor use Something Startling Happens*?*

An editor can use the beats in this book as a minute-by-minute checklist while trimming down a movie. This guide will be a tremendous benefit and timesaver in finding any movie's story rhythm.

How can an actor use Something Startling Happens*?*

Actors are the visual conduit for expressing the all-important minute-by-minute story rhythms to the audience. If an actor fails to touch upon each minute's specific rhythm or benchmark, then the director and audience will feel that something is lacking in his performance. An actor who has the *Something Startling Happens* beats in his arsenal will have a distinct subconscious advantage over actors who don't.

Does Something Startling Happens *work in foreign films as well? Don't the cultural differences affect the beats?*

The beats described in this book apply to *all* successful films, no matter which country they are developed in. Though some of the themes and political concerns may vary from culture to culture, the story rhythms are universal and are at the foundation of every good movie. That's why I included an Akira Kurosawa film, *Rashomon*, as one of the examples. Even though the Japanese culture may be distinctively different from the American, Italian, German, or French cultures, their movie storytelling techniques, at the core, still use the exact same beats.

I don't understand: How can a romantic comedy be the same as a horror movie?

Movies are strikingly similar to architecture. Just as a romantic villa built in a sunflower meadow in Tuscany looks wildly different in appearance to an eerie Transylvania castle once owned by Vlad the Impaler, the architectural principles upon which those uniquely different buildings were designed and constructed are *exactly* the same. So it is with movie stories.

Can I use Something Startling Happens *to write a novel?*

Novelists have the luxury of exploring and expanding upon the inner workings of their characters, and the ability to allow page upon page of bountiful description. Despite this literary freedom, however, their main function is to tell a good story. Since *Something Startling Happens* lays out the consecutive beats of successful storytelling in movies, the novelist can borrow these beats as a guide or checklist, especially if he or she wishes to eventually develop their novel into a feature-length film.

Sometimes when I break down movies, as suggested in your book, the movie I'm studying doesn't show your beats. Why is this?

Successful movies adhere strictly to the minute-by-minute beats, as demonstrated over and over in this book. On rare occasions the beats are slightly early or late (usually within 5 to 20 seconds), but the point is: The beats are there, or at least in the vicinity. If finding the beats is difficult for you, try reviewing Step 2 in *Five Things You Need To Know Before You Begin This Book* (pg. xxi) and re-read *How To Break Down Movies On Your Own* (pg. xxiii) until these concepts become crystal clear in your mind. Just like any skill, you have to master the basics and then practice them until they become second nature.

Can **Something Startling Happens** *be used for graphic novels?*

The beats described in this book would be ideal for the visual medium of graphic novels, especially if the writer pens the story between 70 and 120 pages. In such a case, the minute-by-minute beats could be applied page-by-page, much like a film script.

Can development executives, managers, or agents use this book?

Although there are many astute agents, managers, and development execs in the business, some still struggle to explain exactly what is wrong with a particular script to their clients. While some executives, managers, and agents demonstrate adequate skill at explaining character arc or the requirements of a three-act structure, they can still find it difficult to troubleshoot those numerous pages between major plot points. That's where this book comes in handy: It explores, in depth, all those in-between pages. For example, if you feel that your client's script is lagging during Pages 51–59, you can flip to Minutes 51–59 in this book to see exactly what needs to happen during those pages.

I trust that all of your questions have been answered, or *will* be answered by the time you finish this book. Now let's have some fun while we break down movies minute-by-minute!

IN DA BEGINNING

MINUTE 1: ATTENSION!

Whether it's action, drama, comedy, horror, western, or suspense thriller, all successful movies start with *tension*: Anxiety, apprehension, danger, discomfort, crisis, distress, hostility, or sexual tension. <u>*Tension grabs attention*</u>, as the classic theater adage goes. When you hear the couple arguing in the apartment below you, it grabs your attention. When you see an overturned school bus on the highway, it grabs your attention. Even though you try not to look, a man and woman kissing passionately in a parked car draws your eye (sexual tension). [Other people's tension peaks our curiosity, it yanks us from our everyday existence and injects us with a sudden rush of adrenaline.]

One of the most popular tension-grabbers in film is DANGER. In *Halloween*, someone creeps toward an average-looking house and secretly watches the teenagers make out in the kitchen. In *Jaws*, something ominous moves through the water. In *Knocked Up*, Ben and his friends fight with boxing gloves that are on fire. In *Star Wars*, the opening text warns of Civil War. In *Raiders of the Lost Ark*, Indiana Jones and his crew head deep into a dangerous jungle. In *Scream*, a mysterious stranger calls Casey when she's home by herself.

Minute 1 in *The Sixth Sense*: A sudden basement chill frightens Anna — *Attension*.

When we see something dangerous happening to others, our attention peaks because we feel, deep down, that we have to keep an eye on it for self-preservation. If Ben and his buddies are fighting with on-fire boxing gloves, they could accidentally stumble over to where I'm sitting and catch *me* on fire! So I'd better pay attention. If someone warns of war, I'd better pay attention, because that war could end up in my own backyard, or I may get drafted. If a guy creeps toward someone else's house and peers through their windows, someone could be looking through *my* windows, too.

Another attention grabber is ANXIETY. Most of us do not enjoy feeling anxious, but boy are we intrigued to see others experiencing it. In *Die Hard*'s first minute, John McClane, who's afraid of flying, death-grips the plane's armrest. In *Little Miss Sunshine*, anxious beauty contestants wait to see who will be voted Miss America. In *Spider-Man*, Peter Parker sprints after the bus, anxious because he might be late for school. In *Rashomon*, an angst-ridden commoner says to the priest, "I don't understand."

HOSTILITY also grabs our attention. When we're at the store and we see a customer yelling at the cashier, our eyes snap toward the yeller. Why? Because we're curious how the cashier is going to handle the situation. Will she get the manager? Will she yell back? Hostility comes in two forms: verbal and physical. Say the customer throws a punch at the manager. Now they have our undivided attention — that fight might spill over to my lane and I could get a broken nose. I better keep my eye on the situation.

Another attention grabber is SEXUAL TENSION. Say we're hiking in the woods and we see, in the distance, a naked couple having sex. It immediately grabs our attention, doesn't it? It's something forbidden. It's something we're not supposed to watch, but we're drawn to it. *Basic Instinct*'s first minute begins with a rock star having sex with a beautiful blonde woman in his mansion. We know we shouldn't be looking, but we can't help it.

Their sexual tension creates tension inside us.

UNEASE subtly grabs our attention, too. In *The Godfather*, an uneasy Bonasera tells Don Corleone that boys beat up his daughter. Why is Bonasera uneasy around this guy? Should I be uneasy, too? In *Match Point*, Chris Wilton is uneasy about the randomness of the world. "It's scary to think how much is out of our control," he observes. In *Forrest Gump*, Forrest starts telling his story to a stranger at the bus stop. She has no idea who this odd person is and why he's talking to her, which makes her uneasy.

Now, as case studies, let's look at the first minute of a few wildly different films — *Juno*, *The Matrix*, *Pulp Fiction*, *Being John Malkovich*, and *Halloween* — and see which attention grabber they used. I'll be referencing these case studies throughout the book to prove that the beats consistently work, no matter what genre you choose to write.

Juno uses SEXUAL TENSION to grab us. Juno MacGuff and Paulie Bleeker are about to have sex on his recliner. We've all experienced that awkward first sexual encounter and we're instantly intrigued to see how Juno and Paulie will handle it. Will they be graceful about it, or clumsy? Their sexual tension also ignites those same feelings inside us.

The Matrix and *Pulp Fiction* use DANGER. In *The Matrix*, Cypher tells Trinity, "We're going to kill him." Sounds dangerous. Kill who? Why do they want to kill him? If they kill him, will they also kill me? In *Pulp Fiction*, Pumpkin tells Honey Bunny that robbing the restaurant is "too risky." If we were sitting in the booth behind them and overheard their conversation, our ears would perk up immediately. If they rob the restaurant, they could hurt me, or take my money. I better keep listening to see if they are actually serious.

Being John Malkovich uses ANXIETY during its first minute. The male puppet that Craig manipulates is distressed and anxious about his life. If the puppet is distressed and anxious, will *I* someday become stressed and anxious? I want to know why the puppet is anxious so I can avoid that same miserable feeling.

Halloween uses three-tension-builders-in-one. The hand-held camera, simulating our point of view, makes us UNEASY. Suddenly we are the voyeur, and we're the one who is DANGEROUS. Then, through the creepy person's eyes, we peer into a kitchen window and see teenagers making out — SEXUAL TENSION.

Which type of tension will you choose for your script's first page? Once you figure it out, move to Minute 2.

MINUTE 2: THE BUILD

Not only does....

Audience anticipation is increased by "building upon" already existing tension. Good screenwriters know that opening a story with tension will grab an audience, but just as in real life, if you don't escalate that tension, people will lose interest. If the arguing couple downstairs stops yelling at each other, or the tone of their argument drones on, we soon turn up our TV to drown them out. But if we hear a sudden hard *Slap!* — well, we keep listening, don't we? The tension escalates, and so does our interest.

For example, in *Spider-Man*, after Peter *barely* makes it onto the school bus, how does the screenwriter build tension to keep us interested? By showing the other students refusing to let Peter sit with them. In *Star Wars*, ships fire at each other. In *Knocked Up*, Pete and Debbie argue because Pete can't take the kids to school. In *Being John Malkovich*, the puppet overturns the table.

A great way to help you escalate the tension in your story is to use the phrase, *Not only does....* For example, here's how now-famous movies handled Minute 2:

The Build during Minute 2 of *Raiders of the Lost Ark*: Not only does Indiana Jones find a threatening statue, but he also discovers a deadly arrow.

THE GODFATHER
Not only does Bonasera say that the boys beat his daughter, but he says that she will never be beautiful again.

TOP GUN
Not only does the enemy's plane pursue the American pilots, but now the MiG wants to go head-to-head with Maverick.

JAWS
Not only does a shark swim nearby, but now sexual tension escalates between two nearby college students.

SCREAM
Not only does Casey get a mysterious call from a stranger, but the stranger calls a *third* time.

SPEED
Not only does Payne stab a security guard in the ear, but now executives enter an elevator Payne rigged with explosives.

Now, let's look at the second minute of our case studies and see how they built the tension.

Juno uses URGENCY to build tension. After drinking a lot of Sunny D, Juno desperately has to use the bathroom. And why did she drink all that Sunny D? Because she's taking her third pregnancy test of the day. (*Not only does* Juno desperately have to pee, but now she has to take her third pregnancy test of the day.)

The Matrix uses URGENCY as well. *Not only do* the police break down the door and find Trinity by herself, but now agents show up outside and argue with the Police Chief.

Pulp Fiction uses a THREAT to build tension. In Pumpkin's story, the bank robbers threaten to kill a little girl. (*Not only does* Pumpkin say the robbery is too risky, but now the bank robbers in his story threaten to harm a little girl.)

Being John Malkovich uses FRUSTRATION. The male puppet overturns the table in frustration. (*Not only does* the male puppet pace around his room in distress, but now he flips over the table.)

Halloween uses LIFE THREATENING DANGER. Whoever was watching the teenagers making out now enters the kitchen and grabs a knife. (*Not only does* the stranger enter the kitchen, but now he grabs a sharp blade.)

Now, let's keep the tension rolling into....

MINUTE 3: THE RATCHET

Not only that, but now....

My dad is quite the handyman and taught me how to use a ratchet wrench when I was a teenager. The ratchet was perfect for tightening bolts in small spaces, like inside the engine block of my Chevy Nova. As the ratchet screwed the bolt closer to the metal plate, I could feel the tension escalate in my wrist and forearm. We use that same ratchet principle during Minutes 3 and 4.

Following the hard *Slap!* we heard in the apartment below us, we now hear a loud scream and dishes crashing. The tension builds even more. We want to know what's going to happen next. A great phrase to help you build the tension even more is *Not only that, but now...*. For example:

SPEED
Not only that, but now more cops arrive on the scene.

TOOTSIE
Not only that, but now casting directors reject Michael.

SCREAM
Not only that, but now the caller growls, "Don't hang up on me!"

FORREST GUMP
Not only that, but now young Forrest falls while using his arm braces.

KNOCKED UP
Not only that, but now one of Debbie's daughters said she Googled "murder."

The Ratchet during Minute 3 of *Star Wars*: *Not only that, but now* C-3PO says, "We're doomed."

Anxiety and life-threatening danger seem to be the best ways to build the tension even more. Let's look at our case studies:

Juno uses ANXIETY to build tension. Juno takes the pregnancy test and finds out that she is definitely pregnant — the last thing on earth she wants to be. (*Not only that, but now* she's pregnant.)

—I'm noticing solid sequences that follow the same subject are good when they contain these aspects. Not that each one of these beats needs to be it's own scene.

Being John Malkovich also uses ANXIETY. Craig's wife, Lotte, suggests that Craig get a job — the last thing he wants to do because it will take him away from puppeteering. (*Not only that, but now* Craig's wife wants him to get a job.)

Pulp Fiction uses ANXIETY as well. Pumpkin and Honey Bunny's robbing-the-restaurant debate grows more serious. (*Not only that, but now* Pumpkin and Honey Bunny are talking more seriously about robbing everyone in the restaurant.)

Halloween increases the LIFE THREATENING DANGER. The stranger creeps upstairs with the knife. (*Not only that, but now* the stranger sneaks upstairs with a sharp blade.)

The Matrix increases the LIFE THREATENING DANGER as well. (*Not only that, but now* Morpheus tells Trinity that they've been compromised — agents are outside!)

And don't be afraid to switch the tension to another character besides the hero. For example, in *Spider-Man*, they switch the tension to Harry, who doesn't want his dad to drop him off in front of the school — a tense moment between father and son.

Once you've done that, turn the heat up even more....

MINUTE 4: ANOTHER NOTCH

If you thought that was bad....

After hearing the slap in the downstairs apartment, the boyfriend now screams, "I'm gonna kill you!" We are riveted. What's going to happen next? Should I do something to help? Call the police?

A phrase to help you ratchet up the tension another notch is: *If you thought that was bad....*

RAIDERS OF THE LOST ARK
If you thought that was bad, now Indy's ally pulls a gun on him.

JAWS
If you thought that was bad, now the shark bites the girl and drags her around.

KNOCKED UP
If you thought that was bad, now Sadie conks her sister with the doll and Allison scolds her.

STAR WARS
If you thought that was bad, now Stormtroopers burst through the door.

SCREAM
If you thought that was bad, the caller now threatens to cut Casey like a fish.

TOOTSIE
If you thought that was bad, now Michael is ignored during an audition.

FORREST GUMP
If you thought that was bad, now Forrest's leg brace gets caught in a grate.

How do our case studies ratchet up the tension another notch?

Juno uses the THREAT OF SUICIDE to ratchet the tension. (*If you thought that was bad*, now Juno makes a noose with her string candy.)

The Matrix amps up the LIFE THREATENING DANGER by having the cops chase Trinity onto rooftops, where anyone could fall to their deaths. (*If you thought that was bad*, now cops chase Trinity at death-defying heights.)

Halloween uses DEATH to ratchet the tension. (*If you though that was bad*, now the stranger repeatedly stabs the naked girl.)

Being John Malkovich uses ENVY. (*If you thought that was bad*, now jealous Craig sees another puppeteer having wild television success.)

— these beats are can be minuet but definitly powerful.

Pulp Fiction amps the tension by showing a SYMBOL OF DEATH. (*If you thought that was bad*, now Pumpkin places a handgun onto the table.)

Now that we've built the tension, we need to add a little twist....

All adds up to this →

MINUTE 5: JAW DROPPER

Something extraordinary/astonishing happens.

This minute makes the audience's jaw drop. The story seduces us even further by showing us something extraordinary or astonishing. Things that we don't see or hear every day fascinate us. It grabs our attention and dazzles us. A minute ago, in the downstairs apartment, we heard the boyfriend threaten his girlfriend's life. But what if, during the next minute, we heard a gunshot? This astonishing event would rock our world.

What Jaw Dropper happens in *Jaws*? The shark yanks the naked girl away from the buoy and pulls her underneath the water — an extraordinary event in her life, to say the least.

The Minute 5 Jaw Dropper moment in *Jaws*.

What extraordinary event happens in *Top Gun*? Maverick flies upside down and overtop the enemy's fighter plane — an extraordinary flying feat. What astonishing event happens in *The Sixth Sense*? Anna and Malcolm see a half-naked man standing in their bathroom. What about *Star Wars*? Ominous Darth Vadar enters the story for the first time, an astonishing moment in movie history. *The Godfather*? Bonasera asks Don Corleone to murder the men who beat up his daughter — an extraordinary request to make of someone.

Tootsie? Michael storms out of a play because he disagrees with the director — an extraordinary thing for a struggling actor, who hasn't worked in two years, to do. *Raiders of the Lost Ark*? An extraordinary number of spiders crawl onto Indy and his ally's back. These are all things that would provoke us to say, "Hey, *that's* something you don't see everyday!" In *Rashomon*, the priest says that the story he's about to tell may make the listener lose his faith in the human soul — a jaw-dropping thing for a man of God to say!

How do our case studies drop our jaws in Minute 5?

In *The Matrix*, Trinity executes an extraordinary superhuman leap through a far away window (which astonishes the cops).

In *Halloween*, we find out that the person who stabbed the naked girl is a little boy.

In *Being John Malkovich*, Craig performs a remarkably beautiful puppet performance on the city sidewalk — he has extraordinary talent.

In *Pulp Fiction*, Pumpkin and Honey Bunny hold up the restaurant, an astonishing occurrence in the patrons' lives.

In *Juno*, Juno tells Leah her extraordinary news — she's pregnant. (Leah's jaw literally drops open in astonishment.)

Is something Jaw Dropping happening on Page 5 of your script?

MINUTE 6: FRIEND OR FIST

Hero and ally(s) bond or fight.

You hear the gunshot in the apartment below you. Scared, your eyes flick toward your stunned roommate, who's sitting on the nearby couch. You press your trembling pointer finger against your lips and whisper, "*Shhh!*" Your roommate insists on calling 911, but his cell phone is charging across the room. You don't want the psycho neighbor to know you're home, so you order your roommate to stay still....

These next two minutes are about establishing the hero and ally's relationship. This is a crucial step because the ally plays a big part in the hero's life later on. Because of this fact, we need to get to know him, and the hero, a bit better. Why? So we care what happens between them, and to them, further down the road. The best way to do this is by showing them either bonding (FRIEND) or fighting (FIST). How do the successful movies show the hero and ally bonding during Minute 6?

In *Spider-Man*, Peter encourages Harry to talk with Mary Jane (FRIEND). In *Raiders of the Lost Ark*, Indy saves his ally from falling (FRIEND). In *Jaws*, Brody and his wife joke around (FRIEND). In *Forrest Gump*, Mama Gump reads to young Forrest (FRIEND). In *Little Miss Sunshine*, Sheryl brings her suicidal brother home (FRIEND). In *Top Gun*, Maverick and Goose prepare themselves for an air fight (FRIEND). In *Match Point*, Chris, Tom, and Chloe watch an opera together (FRIEND). In *The Godfather*, Bonasera asks Don Corleone to be his friend (FRIEND). In *Tootsie*, Michael and his roommate chat during their waitering job (FRIEND). In *Speed*, Jack and Detective Harold Temple work together to break into the elevator shaft (FRIEND). In *Scream*, Casey and her tied-up boyfriend make eye contact through the window (FRIEND).

Minute 6 in *Die Hard*: John and his limo driver, Argyle, chat (FRIEND).

And how do successful movies show the hero and ally(s) fighting?

In *Star Wars*, R2-D2 and C-3P0 argue (FIST). In *Knocked Up*, Alison and Ryan Seacrest argue about the next guest (FIST). Alison then offers Ryan a cookie to calm him down (FRIEND).

Our case studies show a variety of ways to show heroes and allies bonding, which seems to be the popular choice for Minute 6.

In *Juno*, Juno's BEST FRIEND, Leah, helps Juno carry the chair (FRIEND). In *Halloween*, Dr. Loomis chats with his AS-SOCIATE, the nurse, on their drive toward the mental hospital (FRIEND). In *Pulp Fiction*, Jules and Vincent, CO-HITMEN, chat in the car about Vincent's recent trip to Europe (FRIEND).

Charlie Kaufman uses a unique angle in *Being John Malkovich* to explore this Minute 6 pattern: The male and female PUPPETS that Craig manipulates long for each other through the wall (FRIEND).

"What about *The Matrix*?" you ask, "Agent Smith can't be the hero, he's the bad guy!" Remember when you first saw *The Matrix*, though? At Minute 6, we knew nothing about The Matrix. As far as we were concerned, the agents were trying to capture a creepy woman (Trinity) who just killed a bunch of cops. Agent Smith is a hero at this point, and his FELLOW AGENTS are his allies in the task (we learn later that they are the bad guys).

And this leads us to....

MINUTE 7: FRIEND OR FIST 2

Hero and/or ally(s) bond or fight more.

There's eerie silence in the apartment below us. What is going to happen next? Your roommate disregards your order to stay put. He tiptoes across the wood floor toward his cell phone. You whisper for him to stop! (FIST.) The floor creaks. You draw in a hiss of breath as your eyes widen in fear....

FIGHTING EXAMPLES

In *Tootsie*, Michael and Jeff argue about Jeff's play (FIST). In *Knocked Up*, Alison and Ryan Seacrest's argument escalates (FIST). In *Top Gun*, Maverick and Goose argue about whether they should land or not (FIST). In *Forrest Gump*, Mama Gump scolds Forrest (FIST).

Minute 7 in *Match Point*: Tom and Chris play tennis (FRIEND).

BONDING EXAMPLES

In *Spider-Man*, Mary Jane smiles and says "yes" when Peter asks to take her picture for the school newspaper (FRIEND). In *Raiders of the Lost Ark*, Indy saves his companion's life... again (FRIEND). In *Jaws*, Mrs. Brody tells her husband to be careful, then his youngest son waves to him (FRIEND). In *The Godfather*, Don Corleone gathers with his wife and children for a family photograph (FRIEND). In *Die Hard*, John continues his friendly chat with Argyle (FRIEND). In *Speed*, Jack and Harold examine the bomb together (FRIEND). In *The Sixth Sense*, Malcolm talks to his former patient in soothing tones (FRIEND).

Need more convincing? Let's see what our case studies do:

In *Juno*, Juno and Leah chat more about Juno having sex with Paulie (FRIEND).

In *The Matrix*, Trinity sends Neo an email, telling him the Matrix has him (FRIEND).

In *Halloween*, Dr. Loomis and the nurse discuss Michael Myers even more (FRIEND).

In *Being John Malkovich*, the young girl's father — who was letting his daughter watch Craig's puppet show (Craig's temporary ally) — punches Craig when he sees the puppets' sexual gestures (FIST).

In *Pulp Fiction*, Jules and Vincent grab guns out of the trunk and chat more (FRIEND).

MINUTE 8: SOMETHING STARTLING HAPPENS

Suddenly, downstairs, the boyfriend kicks open his apartment door. Startled, you spring off the couch and deadbolt your door!

Minute 8 startles somebody in the movie — mostly the hero — and in turn startles the audience. The audience needs a jolt here to keep them awake until the Inciting Incident happens between Pages 10 and 12. The Minute 8 startling event comes in all shapes and sizes. In *Raiders of the Lost Ark*, the crumbling temple *startles* Indy. In *Knocked Up*, Alison's boss *startles* Alison by offering her an on-air job. In *Tootsie*, Michael's friends *startle* him by surprising him with a birthday party. (30 seconds earlier in this case.) In *Jaws*, the gruesome state of the dead girl's body *startles* Brody. In *The Sixth Sense*, the half-naked man *startles* Malcolm by pointing a gun at him and shooting him. In *Scream*, the caller *startles* Casey by gutting her boyfriend. The enormity of his wife's office building *startles* John in *Die Hard*. In *Top Gun*, Maverick is *startled* by the news that Cougar is in trouble.

Minute 8 in *Spider-Man*: The spider bites Peter, which *startles* him.

In *Match Point*, something *startling* happens to middle-class Chris — wealthy Chloe falls in love with him! Something *startling* happens at Don Corleone's daughter's wedding: FBI agents write down license plate numbers in the driveway.

Is something startling happening on Page 8 of your script? You'd better startle the reader, or they're going to get restless here.

What startling event happens in our case studies?

In *Juno*, Juno startles Paulie when she tells him she's pregnant (the startled look on Paulie's face is priceless).

In *Halloween*, an escaped mental patient leaps onto the car and startles the nurse.

In *Pulp Fiction*, Vincent is startled to learn that his boss murdered a man over a simple foot massage.

This startling event not only startles the characters in the movie, but it startles us as well. If we're surprised, we wonder what other surprises await us....

MINUTE 9: THE PURSUIT

Hero discovers something extraordinary/astonishing that must be pursued.

You hear the neighbor stomp up the stairs towards your apartment. He pumps bullets into his shotgun's chamber. Your roommate bolts toward the bathroom to hide. You follow him to safety....

The hero goes into pursuit mode here, and the audience will want to follow if you've properly addressed the steps leading to this minute. Whatever extraordinary thing the hero learns at this beat point, it prods him into action. His action peaks our curiosity — What's going to happen next?

In *Raiders of the Lost Ark*, Indy discovers the astonishing fact that his ally, who's life he saved, is stealing the idol and leaving him to die. Indy *pursues* him. In *Knocked Up*, Alison finds out Debbie caught her husband pleasuring himself. She wants to know more. In *Jaws*, Brody discovers the extraordinary news that the girl died from a shark attack. He must kill the shark. In *Top Gun*, Maverick discovers the extraordinary news that the usually cool-as-a-cucumber Cougar is panicking. Maverick must help him.

In *Spider-Man*, Osborn (who is the hero in this case) discovers the astonishing news that the evil board voted to retest his experiment. He's going to *pursue* another course of action. In *Scream*, Casey catches an astonishing glimpse of the costumed killer. She must grab a knife to protect herself. In *The Sixth Sense*, Malcolm discovers the astonishing fact that his new patient has the same disorder as the man who shot him. He pursues the boy. In *Rashomon*, the commoner finds a dead body (7 seconds later in this case), and must pursue the truth of what happened.

Minute 9 in *Little Miss Sunshine*: Frank discovers the astonishing news that Dwayne won't speak. He must find out why — The Pursuit.

Case studies:

In *Juno*, Juno discovers the astonishing fact that Paulie is cool with her having an abortion. She feels she must pursue that option.

In *The Matrix*, Neo discovers the extraordinary fact that the girl has a white rabbit tattoo on her shoulder. He must pursue her and see where it leads.

In *Halloween*, Dr. Loomis discovers the astonishing news that Michael Myers has escaped. He must pursue him at all costs.

In *Being John Malkovich*, Craig discovers that the hallway ceiling is extraordinarily low. He must find out why.

In *Pulp Fiction*, Jules discovers that Vincent thinks a foot massage is on the same par as oral sex. He must pursue the argument with Jules to discover why.

The key here is that not only do the movies keep us off balance during the story's crucial opening 10 minutes, they throw something at us during Minute 9 that propels the hero, or one of the heroes, forward. This technique draws the reader deeper into the story. If the hero wants to pursue this extraordinary event, so must we....

MINUTE 10: THE DISCUSSION

Someone important to the hero wants to discuss something significant.

The Discussion draws in the audience. When someone important to us — either a lover, boss, parent, sibling, enemy, or friend — approaches us with a serious face and says, "I have something to discuss with you," it tweaks our interest. *What's this important thing they want to talk to me about?*

For example, when the armed boyfriend from downstairs starts ramming his shoulder against your apartment door and growls "Let me in!" — it grabs our attention, right? This neighbor has suddenly become extremely important to us, hasn't he? And what he wants to discuss is significant because it involves our lives. Movie storytellers use this same real-life attention grabber during Minute 10 to keep us interested in their story.

In *Spider-Man*, Uncle Ben and Aunt May (RELATIVES) want to talk to Peter about why he doesn't feel well. In *Raiders of the Lost Ark*, Belloq (ARCH ENEMY) wants to talk to Indy about the idol Indy retrieved. In *Tootsie*, a pretty actress (POTENTIAL LOVER) wants to talk to Michael about an audition. In *Jaws*, the mayor (BOSS) calls after Brody, wanting to know what all the commotion is about (37 seconds later in this case). In *Little Miss Sunshine*, Richard (BROTHER-IN-LAW) wants to talk to Frank about his suicide.

The Discussion during Minute 10 of *Top Gun*: The Chief (BOSS) talks with Maverick about flying back to help Cougar with no fuel left.

In *Match Point*, Chris meets the sensual Nola (POTENTIAL LOVER), who wants to play ping-pong with him. In *Forrest Gump*, Jenny (FRIEND) wants to talk to Forrest about his awkwardness. In *Speed*, Jack and Harold (COWORKER AND FRIEND) discuss why they took this dangerous job. In *Star Wars*, R2-D2 wants to discuss something important with C-3PO (FRIEND).

Who's the "important someone" in our case studies, and what do they want to discuss?

In *Juno*, the jock (CLASSMATE who secretly likes Juno) wants to talk to Juno about her dropped books.

In *The Matrix*, Trinity (POTENTIAL FRIEND) wants to discuss The Matrix with Neo.

In *Halloween*, Laurie's Dad (PARENT) tells her to drop the key off at "the Myers place." (Significant because this is where Michael Myers, the killer, first sees her.)

In *Being John Malkovich*, Dr. Lester (BOSS) interviews Craig for the job. (Significant because this job is where Craig will find the portal).

In *Pulp Fiction*, Jules (COWORKER AND FRIEND) wants to discuss foot massages with Vincent. (Significant to Jules because he's escorting his boss's wife to dinner later that night, and his boss is known to have killed someone who flirted with her.)

NOTE: The Inciting Incident (or "Catalyst") happens between Minutes 10 and 12. The Inciting Incident is an event that upsets the established order in the hero's ordinary world, and ups the stakes. For example, ten minutes into *The Matrix*, Neo meets Trinity face to face for the first time, and she tells him that the answer to "What is the Matrix?" will find him, if he wants it to. This is a big deal in the story — and the first major turning point for the hero. *The Matrix*'s Inciting Incident not only introduces Neo's Love Interest (Trinity), but also touches upon a Major Theme (Free Will vs. Destiny), and the Main Story Question for Act One: Will Neo find "The Matrix"? You don't always have to hit all three of these at once in the Inciting Incident, but you must at least touch upon Act One's Main Story Question.

EXERCISE ONE

Okay, since we're 10 minutes into the film, let's test your skills with two successful movies from different genres. Find the Page 5 JAW DROPPER in Roger Michell's *Notting Hill* and Oliver Stone's *Wall Street*. Hint: After cueing your stopwatch to 1:00 (one minute)*, start your stopwatch when William (Hugh Grant) begins his narration (after Elvis Costello's opening song), and when Bud (Charlie Sheen) steps out of the packed elevator to go to work. These are the moments when both movie stories officially start.

*See the explanation of why you start at 1:00 instead of 0:00 in the section titled *How To Break Down Movies On Your Own* (pg. xxiii).

MINUTE 11: THE WARNING

A warning or threat is made.

As your apartment door starts to give way, the armed boyfriend screams, "Let me in right now!"

When a warning or threat is made to us in real life, we must address it immediately. If someone is threatening us, it could affect our lives in a major way. It could impact our finances, our health, our important relationships, or even our very existence. So it is for the audience, and why The Warning works in the next couple minutes.

In *Jaws*, the deputy *warns* Brody that there are Boy Scouts swimming in the dangerous ocean. In *Top Gun*, the Chief *warns* Maverick that he's already been put on probation three times. In *Match Point*, Nola wants to play ping-pong for a thousand pounds (a *warning* to Chris that he may be hustled). In *Scream*, the killer pulls out a knife (a *warning* that he could kill her).

In *Little Miss Sunshine*, Sheryl *warns* Olive not to ask Frank about his wounds. A friend *warns* Michael not to hit on the married girl in *Tootsie*. In *Forrest Gump*, Jenny's refusal to go home is a *warning* to Forrest that something is wrong.

Minute 11 in *Raiders of the Lost Ark*: Belloq warns Indy to hand over the gun or the Hovitos will kill him.

How do our case studies show a warning or threat?

In *Juno*, Juno and Paulie's lab partners *threaten* each other verbally.

In *The Matrix*, Trinity *warns* Neo: "They are watching you."

In *Halloween*, the ominous atmosphere *warns* of an upcoming threat.

In *Being John Malkovich*, Dr. Lester says to Craig, "We'll see how good you are." (A *warning* to Craig that he may not get hired.)

In *Pulp Fiction*, Jules *warns* Vincent that they should get into character.

MINUTE 12: HARSHER WARNING

A harsher warning or threat is made.

The boyfriend jams his shoulder through your weakening door. The bolt and chain are giving way. "I'm gonna kill you!" he screams....

Someone can warn us, and it'll grab our attention, but if they amp up the warning, we have no choice but to devote our full attention to the problem. The same is true in movie storytelling.

For example, in *Top Gun* the Chief threatens to demote Maverick. In *Spider-Man*, Osborn's assistant *warns* him not to do the test. In *Knocked Up*, the bartender yells at Ben, "Come on, Man!" — a *warning* not to take the beers. In *Little Miss Sunshine*, Sheryl and Grandpa *warn* Richard not to talk about his "9 Steps." In *Speed*, the cable anchor breaks loose — a *threat* of death to the elevator passengers. In *Match Point*, Chloe tells Chris, "Did anyone tell you that you play an aggressive game — a *warning* that he's coming on too strong. Casey tries to *warn* her parents about the killer in *Scream*.

Minute 12 in *Jaws*: The mayor *warns* Brody not to put up the "No Swimming" signs.

Case studies:

In *Juno*, the female lab partner yells and runs off (a *threat* to their RELATIONSHIP).

In *The Matrix*, the boss *warns* Neo not to be late again or he'll be fired (a *threat* to his FINANCIAL SECURITY).

In *Halloween*, the boy *warns* Laurie not to go toward the Myers' house (a *warning* to help preserve Laurie's LIFE).

In *Being John Malkovich*, Craig is offered the job (a *threat* to his puppeteering DREAMS).

In *Pulp Fiction*, Jules *warns* Vincent not to take Marsellus's girlfriend out (a *warning* to help preserve his LIFE).

—the human element →

MINUTE 13: THE SUBMISSION

Final warning/threat is made and the hero submits.

As the boyfriend crashes through your front door, you and your roommate lock yourselves into your tiny bathroom....

Submission gains the audience's sympathy. We all react, subconsciously, when the hero submits. Why? Because we have been there ourselves. How many times have we tucked our tail between our legs and took it from a boss, a spouse, a teacher, a parent, or a traffic cop? It's humiliating. And when this happens to the hero, their weakness makes him real, and gives us an extra reason to cheer for him. Hopefully, down the road, he'll overcome this weakness. And if he doesn't, we'll feel pity for him. Either way, we're on his side.

— this reaction establishes connection

What are the various ways the hero submits to warnings in movies?

BACKS DOWN
In *Jaws*, the mayor warns Brody not to be rash. Brody backs down and complies.

RUNS AWAY
In *Forrest Gump*, when the kids threaten Forrest, he runs away.

STAYS SEATED/REMAINS SILENT
In *Raiders of the Lost Ark*, Indy finds a snake in the plane. Unable to jump out, he sits there, terrified. In *Top Gun*, Commander Jester warns the students that a higher percentage of pilots died in the Vietnam War. The student pilots silently sit and listen. In *Tootsie*, Sandy warns Michael that she can't act. Michael sits, with his feet up, and watches her.

GIVES IN
In *Knocked Up*, Jason demands that Ben go with him to the girls' table. Ben gives in and follows him. In *Little Miss Sunshine*, Frank warns the family not to talk about Frank's suicide, but he gives in and lets them. In *Scream*, Casey, almost dead, gives in and allows the killer to drag her.

WALKS AWAY
In *Match Point*, Tom tells Chris that he's engaged to Nola; Chris walks away from her.

How do our case studies submit to the warning or threat?

In *Juno*, realizing that she must do something soon (her pregnancy is threatening her), Juno submits and calls Planned Parenthood (GIVES IN).

In *The Matrix*, the boss makes a final threat to Neo: "Do I make myself clear?" Neo answers: "Yes" (GIVES IN).

In *Halloween*, Michael Myers steps outside, and Laurie WALKS AWAY.

In *Being John Malkovich*, Craig takes the job offer — a bigger threat to his puppeteering career (GIVES IN).

In *Pulp Fiction*, Jules threatens the boys and they do what he says (GIVE IN).

[handwritten margin note: — whatever their decision it needs to set things into greater motion.]

MINUTE 14: DANGER WATCH

Docile hero watches danger approaching.

Cowering in your bathroom, you see the neighbor's foot-shadows approaching the line of light below the door....

The audience's heart level elevates when they watch danger drawing closer. Once when I was a kid, my cousin Lisa and I hid in the back corner of a walk-in closet during a game of Hide & Seek. When my sister Wendy — the Seeker — opened the closet door and stepped inside to look for us, Lisa became so filled with anxiety when she saw my sister's sneakers stepping toward us that she screamed and gave up our hiding spot. Danger Watch builds anticipation the same way with the audience.

Indy watches Marcus approach with ominous news in *Raiders of the Lost Ark*. In *Knocked Up*, Ben watches as Jason hits on Alison's married sister. In *Jaws*, Brody watches helplessly as tourists swim in the deadly water. In *Top Gun*, a seated Maverick glances at Iceman, who glares at him. In *Little Miss Sunshine*, passive Frank allows his family to verbally bash him for liking another man.

In *The Sixth Sense*, Malcolm leans back helplessly after reading Cole's ominous Latin words. R2-D2 sits helpless as a vacuum sucks him up. In *Spider-Man*, Osborn (the hero in this case) watches as the dangerous green gas approaches his nostrils.

Case studies:

In *Juno*, Juno clams up (REMAINS SILENT) when Brenda asks if she barfed in her urn. (DANGER).

While sitting in his cubicle (STAYS SEATED) in *The Matrix*, Neo sees agents looking in his direction (DANGER).

While in class (STAYS SEATED) in *Halloween*, Laurie notices an ominous car sitting outside of the school (DANGER).

While Craig watches an awful work video (REMAINS SEATED) in *Being John Malkovich*, he notices a sexy coworker (DANGER).

In *Pulp Fiction*, Brett sits still (REMAINS SEATED) while hitman Jules eats his hamburger (DANGER).

MINUTE 15:
WHEW, THAT WAS CLOSE!

Hero experiences a close call while danger approaches.

The boyfriend blasts a hole through your bathroom door. The shotgun pellets strike the tiled wall just above your head....

We've all had that moment when the tractor-trailer almost hit our car; or we almost fell down the steps; or a cop flicks on his lights, but then passes us to catch another speeder instead. We drag the back of our hands across our foreheads and say: *Whew, That Was Close!* The top movie screenwriters use this familiar real-life feeling to make the audience's hearts race faster.

In *Spider-Man*, the green gas almost kills Osborn (WHEW!). In *Jaws*, Brody spots something black in the water — but it's just an old man swimming (WHEW!). In *Knocked Up*, Ben almost blows it with Alison by "doing the dice thing too much" (WHEW!). In *Scream*, Casey's dad almost catches Billy in her bedroom. Billy says "Close call" (WHEW!). In *Match Point*, Chris manages to have sex with Chloe without committing to her completely (WHEW!).

Sometimes a close call is implied instead of shown, like in *Raiders of the Lost Ark*: Indy explains to Marcus that he had the *idol in his hand* — it was *this* close (and we know, from having seen it, that Indy experienced a close call when the Hovitos almost kill him).

Our case studies reveal other *Whew!* moments:

In *Juno*, Juno experiences a close call with Su-Chin, who's picketing the abortion clinic (WHEW!).

In *Halloween*, Michael Myers follows the boy, but luckily for the boy, Michael doesn't attack him (WHEW!).

In *Being John Malkovich*, the sexy coworker ignores Craig's sexual advances (sexual close call — WHEW!).

In *Pulp Fiction*, Jules yells at Marvin, but doesn't kill him (WHEW!).

Minute 15 in *The Matrix*: Neo *barely* dodges the agents as he scurries toward the empty office — Whew, That Was Close!

MINUTE 16: THE BIG CONCERN

Glancing at the ragged bullet hole just above your head, your eyes widen with fear. Terrified, your roommate pees his pants....

The definition of The Big Concern is: *A troubled or anxious state of mind.* Whatever causes The Big Concern must be addressed immediately, which is a writer's secret weapon to slingshot the story forward. In some cases the hero is the one who shows concern:

In *Scream*, Sidney expresses concern when Billy's hand drifts too far up her skirt. In *Raiders of the Lost Ark*, Indy shows concern when he learns that army intelligence has come to see him. "Am I in trouble?" he asks Marcus. In *Jaws*, Brody is concerned about going into the water. In *Knocked Up*, Ben shows concern because he can't get his condom on. In *Speed*, Jack expresses concern because the bomber may still be in the building. And in *Rashomon*, the bandit shows concern as he begins to tell his side of the story.

In some cases the ally shows concern:

In *Spider-Man*, Aunt May is concerned that Peter will be late. Sheryl shows concern when Richard tells his daughter about the "9 Steps" in *Little Miss Sunshine*.

Minute 16 in *Tootsie*: Concerned that she won't get to audition, Sandy starts to cry.

In *The Godfather*, Mama shows concern when she's asked to sing. In *Top Gun*, Goose is concerned because Iceman may be the best. Eleanor expresses concern over her children's relationships in *Match Point*. In *The Sixth Sense*, Cole's mom shows concern when she discovers that all of the cupboard doors are suddenly open. In *Forrest Gump*, Jenny is concerned her father will find her. Holly shows concern when John brings up her name change in *Die Hard*.

Who's showing concern during Minute 16 in our case studies?

In *Juno*, the receptionist thinks Juno is lying about her age (which causes Juno concern).

In *The Matrix*, Neo is concerned that he might go to jail.

In *Halloween*, the boy shows concern after being tripped by the bullies.

In *Being John Malkovich*, Lotte's request to have a baby causes Craig concern.

In *Pulp Fiction*, Brett shows great concern when Jules shoots his friend.

MINUTE 17: WORLD UPSIDE DOWN

Bad guy turns a good person's world upside down.

The psycho boyfriend inserts his shotgun barrel through the hole in the bathroom door and squeezes the trigger. The blast drives your roommate against the wall. You scream!

The World Upside Down moment is when you've been minding your own business and someone comes along and ruins your day. A school bully trips you in the hall. A driver, not paying attention, smashes into your back bumper. A cop pulls you over for rolling through a stop sign. When the bad guy

Minute 17 in *The Sixth Sense*: Cole's mean classmate calls him a "freak" — World Upside Down.

picks on someone on the big screen, [it draws the audience's sympathy and we become even more invested in the story.]

The shark eats the dog and the boy in *Jaws*. In *Spider-Man*, Mary Jane's dad (the bad guy in her eyes) yells at her. Government agents tell Indy that Hitler (the bad guy) is looking for an important artifact. In *Top Gun*, Iceman (the bad guy in this scene) tells Maverick, "You were lucky to get into Top Gun." In *Scream*, Casey plays the momentary bad guy by naughtily flashing her breast, which turns nice-guy Billy's world upside down.

Richard (the bad guy in this scene) tells his wife that they can't take Olive to the contest in *Little Miss Sunshine*. In *The God-father*, Sonny (the bad guy during this minute) takes a young girl upstairs to have a fling. In *Match Point*, Chloe (who's the bad guy in this case) tells Chris that her wealthy father wants to offer him a job (a job he doesn't want).

Bad guy Ben, in *Knocked Up*, has sex with Alison without a condom. In *Star Wars*, the sand creatures lead the droids outside to be sold. The bomber shoots at Jack and Harold in *Speed*. In *Forrest Gump*, the bad guys chase Forrest. In *Die*

Hard, the bad guys show up in the black van, which will soon turn the receptionist's life upside down. In *Tootsie*, Michael's agent (the bad guy in this case) didn't get Michael the acting job he promised him.

How is the good guy's world turned upside down in our case studies?

In *Juno*, the other pregnant patients (BAD GUYS) unnerve Juno (GOOD GUY).

In *The Matrix*, agents (BAD GUYS) handcuff Neo (GOOD GUY) and force him into their car.

In *Halloween*, Michael Myers (BAD GUY) pulls his car next to the boy (GOOD GUY) and watches him walk.

In *Being John Malkovich*, sexy Maxine (BAD GUY) tells Craig (GOOD GUY) that he wouldn't know what to do with her if he got her.

In *Pulp Fiction*, Jules (BAD GUY) shoots Brett's shoulder (GOOD GUY). (The good guy/bad guy roles switch in this case.)

MINUTE 18: TROUBLE TURN

The event that will get the hero into trouble later.

As the psycho boyfriend reloads his double-barrel shotgun, you realize, to your horror, that your roommate is dead. You scramble up onto the bathtub and frantically try to scurry out the window. But as you do, the neighbor shoots at you. Pellets strike your heel....

Trouble Turn is something that will get the hero deeper into a predicament, especially later. The deeper into trouble he gets, the more the audience feels for him. The more they feel for him, the more they'll follow him through every other twist and turn.

Minute 18 in *Spider-Man*: Peter's palm sticks to the bus poster, the beginning of his superpowers, which will get him into trouble later – Trouble Turn.

In *Raiders of the Lost Ark*, Indy learns that Hitler wants the ark so he can obtain great power (which will get Indy into trouble later). In *Jaws*, the victim's bloody floating device washes ashore (which will soon get Chief Brody into trouble). In *Top Gun*, Maverick sees Charlotte for the first time (the woman who will cause him a lot of trouble later). In *The Sixth Sense*, Malcolm shows up at Cole's house for a second session (a choice that will get him into trouble later). In *Scream*, Casey discovers that two teenagers were brutally murdered (news that will affect her deeply later).

Chris considers taking the job in *Match Point*, getting more deeply involved with Chloe, whom he doesn't love. In *Little Miss Sunshine*, Richard, who tries to get out of taking Olive to the contest, runs out of options (which will get him into trouble later). In *The Godfather*, Michael doesn't answer Kate's question about how his father helped Johnny Fontaine (a decision that will get him into trouble later). In *Knocked Up*, Ben realizes that he had drunk-sex with Alison the night before (a decision that will get him into trouble later).

In *Star Wars*, Luke meets R2-D2 and C-3PO (the duo who will get him into trouble later). In *Die Hard*, the bad guys shoot the receptionist and take over the building (which will get John into trouble later). In *Speed*, Jack discovers that the bomber rigged his own body with explosives (his insane behavior will get Jack into trouble later).

What's the Trouble Turn in our case studies?

In *Juno*, Juno decides to stay pregnant.

In *The Matrix*, Agent Smith tells Neo they know he's a computer hacker.

In *Halloween*, Dr. Loomis doesn't notice the dead body in the grass.

In *Being John Malkovich*, Dr. Lester mistakenly scolds Craig for toying with Floris.

In *Pulp Fiction*, Jules shouts a Bible verse at Brett (the verse he always recites just before he kills people).

MINUTE 19: THE THREAT

Bad guy, or secondary bad guys, make a threat/warning.

As you fall hard onto the grass with your wounded heel, you scramble to your feet. You're in deep trouble because the converted two-story house you live in was built in a secluded area of the countryside. You hobble toward the road in hopes of flagging down a rare passing car. Suddenly, the psycho neighbor descends the outside steps, calls your name and yells, "No use runnin'! You're eventually goin' down!" (Not only are *you* off and running, *your story* is off and running as well....)

The Threat, especially posed by a bad guy who's intent is to harm the hero, draws our audience's attention. Why is this? Because their sympathy for the hero has deepened by this point. They care what happens to him because of the sympathy you've established for him earlier. Let's look at the various types of bad guys who make threats during Minute 19.

Sometimes the bad guy is an OBVIOUS BAD GUY:
In *Raiders of the Lost Ark*, the Nazis (obvious bad guys) threaten to find the Ra headpiece first. In *Die Hard*, the bad guy shoots another innocent employee (obvious bad guy). In *Speed*, the bomber (obvious bad guy) says to Jack, "There will come a time where you'll wish you'd never met me."

Sometimes the bad guy is an INANIMATE OBJECT:
In *Scream*, the empty classroom chair — that a now-dead student once occupied — warns Sidney of impending danger.

In some cases a FAMILY MEMBER temporarily takes on the role of the bad guy:
In *Little Miss Sunshine*, Sheryl says that they can't go without Frank and Dwayne (Sheryl is perceived as the bad guy in this case because she threatens the trip). In *The Godfather*, Kate insists that Michael tell her the truth (she's perceived as the bad guy in this case). In *Knocked Up*, Pete, playing the bad boy during this minute, warns his daughter to "never do what they did." In *Star Wars*, Uncle Owen threatens Luke to get his chores done.

Sometimes the bad guy is an ALTER EGO:
In *Spider-Man*, Green Goblin warns Osborn that something bad will happen.

Sometimes a SUPPOSED FRIEND temporarily takes on the role of the bad guy:
In *Top Gun*, Maverick pretends to be a mischievous bad guy as he playfully warns Charlotte by singing "You've Lost That Lovin' Feelin'." Cole eyes Malcolm suspiciously in *The Sixth Sense* (Cole sees Malcolm as a threat because Malcolm is dead, but the audience doesn't know this yet). In *Match Point*, Nola shows up with Tom for a double date. Nola's presence threatens

— adds a moment of tension.

(an illude to a bigger problem that fleshes out the world.)

Chris and Chloe's relationship. In *Tootsie*, Michael's agent warns Michael that no one will hire him. In *Jaws*, local business owners (whom Brody thought were friends) murmur (threaten) under their breaths that he'd better not close down the beaches.

Other times it's an OPPOSING TEAM PLAYER:

The Threat during Minute 19 in *Forrest Gump*: The opposing football team tries to tackle Forrest.

Which bad guy type did our case studies use?

In *Juno*, Juno finds the *PennySaver* ads (INANIMATE OBJECT) threatening because she wants to give her baby to a worthy couple.

In *The Matrix*, Agent Smith (OBVIOUS BAD GUY) warns Neo that he'd better help them bring Morpheus to justice.

In *Halloween*, Michael Myers (OBVIOUS BAD GUY) drives his car slowly past Laurie and her friends (22 seconds later in this case).

In *Being John Malkovich*, Maxine (SUPPOSED FRIEND) shows up (a threat to Craig's marriage).

In *Pulp Fiction*, Jules and Vincent (OBVIOUS BAD GUYS) shoot Brett.

MINUTE 20: PUSH BACK

Bad people or circumstances, to this point, have been pushing around the hero. Now it's time for him to push back. It shows that he has a bit of a backbone, which gains the audience's respect. They'll find themselves saying, "Good for you!"

Most times ANGER is the emotion the hero evokes during Minute 20:
In *Spider-Man*, Peter hits Mary Jane's boyfriend with his tray. In *Jaws*, Brody tells the business owners he's going to close the beach, which angers them. Dwayne pounds his fist in *Little Miss Sunshine*. In *Tootsie*, Michael angers his agent. In *Speed*, Jack shoots Harold's leg, which makes him swear.

KNOWLEDGE is another way the hero pushes back:
In *Raiders of the Lost Ark*, Indy — who was intimidated by Belloq, the snakes, and now the agents — pushes back intellectually with his superior knowledge of the ark.

The hero can push back by FLIRTING:
Maverick flirts with Charlotte in *Top Gun*.

The hero can push back with a CONTRARY ACTION:
Forrest picks up the black girl's book in front of the disapproving onlookers in *Forrest Gump*. (sympathy)

The hero can push back by saying something SHOCKING:
In *The Godfather*, Michael shocks Kate when he says that his father threatened to kill somebody. In *Scream*, Casey shocks her friends when she asks how to gut someone (3 seconds later in this case).

How does the hero Push Back in our case studies?

[handwritten marginalia:] — How they react to all the shit leading up to this is their core character. It can ger us to respect them or sympathize

Minute 20 in *The Matrix*: Neo gives the agent the finger — The Push Back.

In *Juno*, Paulie expresses his feelings for Juno to his disapproving mother.

In *Halloween*, Annie shouts at Michael Myers, who drives slowly by.

In *Being John Malkovich*, Craig annoys Maxine.

In *Pulp Fiction*, Butch remains stubbornly silent in front of Marsellus.

EXERCISE TWO

In this exercise I'd like you to find Minute 16's Big Concern. For this one we'll use Rob Reiner's *Stand By Me* and Phil Alden Robinson's *Sneakers*. Stopwatch Hint: For *Sneakers*, the movie starts when college-aged Bishop and Cosmo begin their dialogue after the snowy exterior shot (for a short cut, go to the scene where the agents offer to pay adult Bishop [Robert Redford] $175,000). In *Stand By Me*, the story starts as we close in on the truck that the Richard Dreyfuss character is sitting in (for a short cut, The Big Concern happens right after the boys sing "The Ballad of Paladin" on the railroad tracks).

UPPIN' THE ANGST

MINUTE 21: THE GREAT AFFECT

Something happens that greatly affects the hero.

The Great Affect is an action that affects the hero in a positive, negative, or double-edged (positive and negative combined) way:

POSITIVE

In *Match Point*, Nola glances at Chris in a suggestive manner. (Exactly what Chris hoped for.) In *Forrest Gump*, one bus passenger leaves and another sits beside Forrest. (This is good for Forrest because he can continue his story.) During the game in *The Sixth Sense*, Cole steps toward Marcus. (Exactly what Marcus wanted. He can now help the boy.)

NEGATIVE

In *Top Gun*, Charlotte turns Maverick down. In *Scream*, Stuart describes how to gut someone, which makes Sidney cringe. In *Knocked Up*, Alison thinks Ben is a loser for starting a celebrity porn website. In *Die Hard*, the bad guys take over the office building.

DOUBLE-EDGED

In *Speed*, the mayor awards the "Medal of Valor" to Jack, which the bomber watches on TV. In *Tootsie*, Michael goes to an audition, but has to dress as a woman. In *Little Miss Sunshine*, Richard tells Olive they're not going to take her unless she thinks she can win. In *Star Wars*, Luke sees Leia's hologram message, but she reveals bad news. In *Spider-Man*, Mary Jane's boyfriend throws a punch at Peter, but he dodges it easily. In *Jaws*, Quint says he'll capture the shark, but for ten grand.

The Great Affect during Minute 21 in *Raiders of the Lost Ark*: Marcus tells Indy that the government wants him to find the ark, which greatly affects Indy's life.

In *Juno*, Juno tells her parents she's pregnant (DOUBLE-EDGED — it's negative news for her parents, but now they can help her).

In *The Matrix*, the agents insert an electronic bug into Neo's navel (NEGATIVE).

In *Halloween*, the girls talk about keeping each other company tonight (DOUBLE-EDGED — this sounds great to Laurie now, but later Michael Myers will attempt to kill them all).

Losing the bet, Maxine tells Craig she'll meet him for a drink (DOUBLE-EDGED — positive for Craig now, but dangerous for his marriage) in *Being John Malkovich*.

In *Pulp Fiction*, Marsellus gives Butch a large sum of money to throw the fight (DOUBLE-EDGE — positive for his financial situation, but negative for his pride).

MINUTE 22: TRUTH DECLARED

This is the moment of truth, literally. It could be the bad guy, the hero, or the ally, but someone speaks a truth during Minute 22. Why does Truth Declared have a strong affect on storytelling?

Because in our everyday world, we're so inundated with white lies and fluff that when someone speaks the truth, our ears immediately perk up. Advertisers lie to us, as do politicians and sales people. Sometimes even bosses, lovers and friends tell us untruths. Because it is so rare, truth has power. And so it will in your story and to your audience.

"The ark holds many secrets and has great power," Marcus tells Indy in *Raiders of the Lost Ark*. "Faith is the path of least resistance," Chris says in *Match Point*. "Welcome to hell," Dwayne writes to Frank in *Little Miss Sunshine*. "That was fuckin' brutal," Ben says after his disastrous breakfast with Alison in *Knocked Up*. "She's a person of some importance," C-3PO says to Luke about Leia in *Star Wars*. "Dorothy" (Michael's invented female persona) calls the soap director "a macho shithead" in *Tootsie*.

What truth is declared in our case studies?

In *Juno*, Juno declares, "I'm not ready to be a mom."

In *The Matrix*, Morpheus calls Neo "The One."

"The guy you yelled at is behind the bush," Laurie says to Annie in *Halloween*.

In *Being John Malkovich*, Craig tells Maxine that he likes her.

In *Pulp Fiction*, Butch says (about taking the money), "I have no problem with that, Mr. Wallace."

What truth is declared during Page 22 of your script?

MINUTE 23: SCARY STUFF

Hero experiences something scary with ally or love interest.

When Scary Stuff happens to the hero and those he cares about, it scares the audience as well. Why? Because the hero is playing proxy for the audience by this point. It's almost a 50/50 split whether it's an ally or love interest who experiences something scary with the hero during this minute. Either way, the scariness amplifies in intensity over the next three minutes....

ALLY

While working with her editor in *Knocked Up*, Alison watches herself throw up on the video (scary for her because she's trying to hide her pregnancy). In *Little Miss Sunshine*, Grandpa's sex talk scares Richard. In *Spider-Man*, something scary grows out of Peter's fingertips (his hands are his ally at this point). In *Raiders of the Lost Ark*, Indy shows Marcus (ally) his (scary) gun. In *The Sixth Sense*, Cole (ally) tells Malcolm, "You're nice but you can't help me" (scary words for Malcolm). In *Scream*, Casey walks alone (scary) inside her house (her ally).

LOVE INTEREST

In *Match Point*, Chris gives Chloe a gift, which makes her fall more in love with him (scary for him because he's getting more entrenched in her wealthy world). In *Top Gun*, Maverick discovers Charlotte is one of his instructors (scary for his career). In *Forrest Gump*, Forrest sees a man hurting Jenny; he runs to save her (scary situation for him). In *Die Hard*, John hears scary gunshots, so does Holly. In *Tootsie*, Julie helps Michael pick up his dropped script pages (scary for him because he's new at work). In *The Godfather*, Sonny almost gets caught having sex with a young girl (scary because he's married).

During Minute 23 in *Jaws*: Brody's wife (love interest) scares him while he's reading his shark book.

What's scary in our case studies?

Juno and her parents (ALLIES) are unsure how to handle her (scary) pregnancy.

Neo steps into the car with Trinity (ALLY/LOVE INTEREST) and Switch points a gun at him (scary).

In *Halloween*, Laurie walks toward Annie (ALLY) to see if scary Michael Myers is still hiding behind the bush.

In *Being John Malkovich*, Craig lies to Lotte (ALLY/LOVE INTEREST) about where he was (scary for him because he was with Maxine).

In *Pulp Fiction*, Vincent is concerned (scary situation) about his "date" with Marsellus's wife (LOVE INTEREST).

MINUTE 24: SCARY STUFF 2

Hero and/or ally/love interest experience more scary stuff.

During Minute 24, the scariness amps up a notch to hold our audience's attention. Here's how our movie examples do it:

ALLY

In *Spider-Man*, Peter stands atop a scary high ledge. In *Scream*, Sidney sees her dead mother's photo (scary) on the TV news. In *Little Miss Sunshine*, Richard yells at Grandpa for offering Dwayne sex advice (scary for a father to hear). In *The Godfather*, Don Corleone tells his nephew to act like a man. (The Godfather's sudden anger scares Johnny.) In *Knocked Up*, Alison thinks that she might be pregnant (scary situation). In *Star Wars*, Uncle Owen and his wife exchange concerned glances when Luke mentions Obi-Wan (they're scared Luke might find out who he is). In *Die Hard*, the bad guys fire guns near the employees (scary). In *Tootsie*, Michael doesn't know which way to turn his head for the cameras (scary because he might lose his acting job). In *Speed*, a friend tells Jack, "Last time I partied like that I woke up married" (scary idea for bachelor Jack).

LOVE INTEREST

In *Raiders of the Lost Ark*, Marion (Indy's love interest) is involved in an intense drinking game with a large local (scary for her because she might lose her reputation as a woman who can hold her liquor). After viewing scary shark-attack photos, Brody and his wife yell for their son to get out of the boat (they are scared for their son's life) in *Jaws*. In *Top Gun*, Maverick contradicts Charlotte in class (scary for Charlotte who's trying to prove herself). In *The Sixth Sense*, Anna acts cold toward Malcolm at dinner (scary for Malcolm because he wants to reconcile with her). In *Forrest Gump*, Jenny takes off her shirt in front of Forrest and asks if he's ever been with a girl (scary for virgin-Forrest).

What's scary in our case studies?

In *Juno*, Dad (ALLY) scolds Juno (scary for her), "I thought you were the type of girl who knew when to say when."

In *The Matrix*, Trinity (ALLY/LOVE INTEREST) pulls out a scary contraption and presses it onto Neo's navel.

In *Halloween*, Laurie bumps into Sheriff Brackett (ALLY) and screams.

In *Being John Malkovich*, Lotte (ALLY/LOVE INTEREST) gives Craig the cold shoulder (scary for him because he might lose her).

In *Pulp Fiction*, Butch sees the guy he just threatened (Vincent) hug Marsellus (current ALLY in the boxing scam).

MINUTE 25: SCARY STUFF 3

Hero and/or ally/love interest experience even more scary stuff.

In our trilogy of scary minutes, the scariness escalates.

ALLY

In *Spider-Man*, Peter slams into the wall (scary because he may have hurt himself). In *Jaws*, Brody studies his scary shark book even more. In *Top Gun*, the other pilots refuse to believe Maverick flew upside down and gave the MiG pilot the finger (scary for his credibility). In *Scream*, night falls and Casey is alone in her house. In *Little Miss Sunshine*, Olive wants to know what the adults are talking about (a scary moment for the parents). In *Match Point*, Nola doesn't show up for the movie. In *Star Wars*, Uncle Owen tells Luke he must stay for another year, which causes Luke great distress. In *Die Hard*, the head of the bad guys, Hans Gruber, speaks in threatening tones to the employees. In *Tootsie*, Michael may not get the part. In *Speed*, Jack sees a bus blow up.

Minute 25 in *The Sixth Sense*: Anna leaves Malcolm during dinner (scary for Malcolm because he wants to win her back) — Scary Stuff 3.

LOVE INTEREST

In *The Godfather*, Michael pulls Kate into the family picture (something she is scared to do). In *Knocked Up*, Alison is scared because she may have to marry loser Ben. In *Forrest Gump*, Jenny puts Forrest's hand on her breast (scary for him).

How about our case studies?

In *Juno*, Juno and her dad (ALLY) drive to meet the possible adoptive couple (scary situation for Juno).

In *The Matrix*, Trinity's (ALLY/LOVE INTEREST) scary contraption sucks the electronic bug out of Neo's navel.

Standing inside her house (ALLY), Laurie sees scary Michael Myers outside in *Halloween*.

In *Being John Malkovich*, Craig flirts with puppet-Maxine (LOVE INTEREST) in the basement (he's scared his wife might find out).

In *Pulp Fiction*, Vincent and Lance (ALLY) discuss an illegal (scary) heroin purchase.

MINUTE 26: THE BIG UNEXPECTED

A classic example of The Big Unexpected is when Indy enters Marion's bar in *Raiders of the Lost Ark*. She laughs, brushes off her hands and says, "Indiana Jones, I always knew some day you'd come walking back through my door." We think everything is cool between them, so does Indy, when suddenly she *punches* him in the face! Big and unexpected! Before this minute we experienced three minutes straight of scary tension. There has to be an unexpected moment here to keep the audience off balance.

In *Scream*, the killer calls Sidney! Another unexpected call happens in *Speed* when the bomber calls Jack. In *Little Miss Sunshine*, Richard tells Frank to shut up! In *The Godfather*, Don Corleone orders a bunch of killings during his daughter's wedding — last thing you'd expect at someone's nuptials. In *Spider-Man*, Mary

Jane catches Peter listening to her and her father arguing (she didn't expect that). In *Top Gun*, Maverick does the unexpected and blows off Charlotte's request.

Minute 26 in *Raiders of the Lost Ark:* Marion punches Indiana Jones in the face, a classic demonstration of The Big Unexpected.

In *The Sixth Sense*, Cole's mom notices that there are bright orbs in all of Cole's photos (big and unexpected). In *Match Point*, Chris runs into Nola, unexpectedly, on the street. In *Star Wars*, Luke discovers that R2-D2 has left! In *Die Hard*, Takagi unexpectedly reveals he's the company's owner. In *Tootsie*, Michael, dressed as a woman, stuns his agent (who didn't expect such a thing).

What big and unexpected event happens in our case studies?

In *Juno*, Juno stuns Vanessa by telling her she found her ad in the *PennySaver*!

In *The Matrix*, Neo meets the legendary Morpheus in person!

In *Halloween*, the silent caller scares Laurie with another unexpected phone call!

In *Being John Malkovich*, puppet-Maxine unexpectedly kisses puppet-Craig!

In *Pulp Fiction*, Vincent unexpectedly buys three grand worth of heroin!

MINUTE 27: THE MINI-QUEST

Hero embarks on a small, preliminary quest.

Now that we've jolted the audience, let's take them on a Mini-Quest before Act Two's Big Quest begins. This Mini-Quest involves something that is immediately important to the hero or ally. The Mini-Quest's undertone is urgency.

For example, in *Raiders of the Lost Ark*, Indy tells Marion that he needs the bronze medallion (Indy's Mini-Quest before searching for the ark). In *Jaws*, the fisherman tries to swim to shore before the shark eats him (the fisherman's Mini-Quest before all the fishermen try to capture the shark). In *Top Gun*, Maverick must defeat the instructor during the first training exercise (Maverick's Mini-Quest before battling the real bad guys). In *The Sixth Sense*, Cole's mom wants to know what the illuminations are in Cole's photos (her Mini-Quest before discovering her son's unique abilities). In *Scream*, Sidney must find out where the killer is (Sidney's Mini-Quest before finding out the killer's identity).

During Minute 27 in *Match Point*: Chris says he'll walk with Nola to her audition (Chris's Mini-Quest before starting an affair with her).

In *Little Miss Sunshine*, Richard wants Olive to resist ice cream so she doesn't get fat (Richard's Mini-Quest before taking her to the contest). In *The Godfather*, Tom flies to L.A. to talk to the producer about giving Johnny the part (Tom's Mini-Quest before he helps fight the other crime families). In *Knocked Up*, Debbie thinks Alison should call Ben and let him know about her condition (Debbie's Mini-Quest before her sister's pregnancy advances). In *Star Wars*, Luke has to find R2-D2 (Luke's Mini-Quest before he heads off to battle the Death Star).

In *Forrest Gump*, Forrest stands in line to meet President Kennedy (Forrest's Mini-Quest before he searches for Jenny). In *Die Hard*, Hans leads Takagi to the elevator to take him to his office (Hans's Mini-Quest before trying to get the money in the vault). In *Tootsie*, Michael wants to tell his agent he got the soap opera job (Michael's Mini-Quest before he attempts to fool everyone that he's a woman).

Now, what is the Mini-Quest for our case studies?

In *Juno*, Juno and the potential adoptive couple must find out if they are a good fit (their Mini-Quest before they officially adopt the baby).

In *The Matrix*, Neo wants to be told what the Matrix is (Neo's Mini-Quest before he actually sees it).

In *Halloween*, Laurie waits for Annie to pick her up (Laurie's Mini-Quest before she starts her babysitting job).

In *Being John Malkovich*, Craig needs to find the paper he dropped behind the cabinet (his Mini-Quest before he finds the portal).

In *Pulp Fiction*, Vincent looks for his money while Lance gets the drugs (Vince's Mini-Quest before his date with Marsellus's wife).

MINUTE 28: BIG QUEST PREP

Hero prepares for a bigger quest with ally.

Now that the Mini-Quest has been taken care of, or just about been taken care of, it's time for the hero to make preparations for Act Two's Big Quest. And if you've done your job correctly up to this point, the audience will follow the hero on this bigger quest. They'll want to know how he'll fair in this new endeavor. This develops over the next two minutes…

For instance, in *Top Gun*, Maverick and his instructor try to out-maneuver each other (to prepare Maverick to fight the real enemy). In *Spider-Man*, Peter tells Mary Jane he sees something coming he's never felt before (preparing himself to be a super-hero). In *The Sixth Sense*, Malcolm asks Cole questions about his dad (to prepare him to talk about his deeper issues). In *Scream*, Sidney searches around the outside of her house (to prepare herself to survive).

In *Little Miss Sunshine*, Olive decides to take her father's advice and resist the ice cream (to prepare herself for the contest). In *Match Point*, Chloe asks Chris to get a drink (where they will prepare to begin a secret relationship together). Alison asks Ben to get together in *Knocked Up* (to prepare him for the pregnancy). In *Star Wars*, Luke drives the land cruiser to look for R2-D2 (he needs him for the Big Quest).

In *Forrest Gump*, Forrest prepares to go to boot camp with Bubba. In *Die Hard*, John, gun in hand, prepares to fight the bad guys. In *Tootsie*, Michael asks for a loan until pay day (so he can concentrate on acting instead of bills). In *Speed*, Jack — in preparation for the Big Quest — drives a truck to where the bomb-rigged bus is.

Case study preparations:

In *Juno*, Juno negotiates with Vanessa and Mark about what to do when the baby is born.

In *The Matrix*, Morpheus explains to Neo that he has to see The Matrix (preparing him to be The One).

In *Halloween*, Dr. Loomis searches for Judith Myers' grave (preparing himself to find Michael Myers).

In *Being John Malkovich*, Craig opens the small hidden door and taps the walls with a board (the board is his ally in this case. He uses it to prepare for his big adventure inside John Malkovich's mind).

In *Pulp Fiction*, Vincent gets high (prepares himself for his date) and drives to pick up Marsellus's wife.

MINUTE 29: BIG QUEST PREP 2

Hero and/or ally's preparation for bigger quest continues.

A good example of this is when Mary Jane tells Peter not to hunch (preparing him to be a confident man) in *Spider-Man*. Another example is when Sidney relocks her front door in *Scream* (to prepare herself for survival). In *Raiders of the Lost Ark*, Nazis enter Marion's bar (in preparation to take over the medallion so they can find the ark). In *Jaws*, Hooper tries to find Brody (so they can prepare to kill the shark). In *Top Gun*, Maverick beats the instructor (in preparation to beat the real enemy). In *The Sixth Sense*, Malcolm explains free-association writing to Cole (to prepare him to explain why he wrote such horrible things).

Tom, the Corleone family's ally, prepares the producer even further to let Johnny take over the movie's lead role. In *Match Point*, Chris and Chloe flirt over drinks, preparing themselves for their affair. In *Knocked Up*, Alison and Ben meet at the restaurant, preparing themselves to deal with the pregnancy. In *Star Wars*, Luke fights a sand person, preparing himself to fight stronger opponents later. In *Forrest Gump*, Forrest and Bubba talk on the bus, preparing themselves to be best friends. In *Speed*, Jack drives a truck closer to where the bus is, preparing himself to board it.

Minute 29 in *Tootsie*: Michael and Jeff discuss Michael's upcoming soap opera job, preparing him to take on this difficult task — Big Quest Prep 2.

How do the preparations continue in our case studies?

Preparing herself to give her child to Vanessa and Mark, Juno continues to negotiate with them in *Juno*.

In *The Matrix*, Morpheus offers Neo the red or blue pill (preparing him to see The Matrix).

In *Halloween*, Dr. Loomis discovers that Judith Myers' headstone is gone (preparing himself to find Michael Myers).

In *Being John Malkovich*, Craig crawls further into the hole (preparing himself to enter John Malkovich's mind).

In *Pulp Fiction*, Vincent drives to Mia's house and walks to her door (preparing himself to go on their date).

MINUTE 30: THE NEED

The definition of The Need is: *A condition requiring relief; anything that is necessary but lacking.* When we have a need in our life, whether it's to buy some fast food because we're starving, a need to be on time for a job interview, or a need to pursue a love interest, that need becomes our main focus. When the characters in our story express a need, we pay attention because we know the feeling oh too well.

As if on cue, the need is expressed during Minute 30, just when Act Two usually kicks in:

Minute 30 in *Spider-Man*: Peter *needs* to have a brand new car to win over Mary Jane.

In *Speed*, Jack *needs* to find the bus quickly. In *Raiders of the Lost Ark*, the Nazi *needs* to see the medallion. In *Jaws*, Hooper *needs* to examine the victim's remains. In *The Sixth Sense*, Cole *needs* to not be scared anymore. In *Scream*, Sidney *needs* to call the police. In *Little Miss Sunshine*, Richard *needs* a new clutch so he can drive the family to the contest. In *The Godfather*, Tom *needs* to get Johnny into the movie.

In *Match Point*, Chris *needs* Nola sexually. Alison *needs* to tell Ben she's pregnant in *Knocked Up*. In *Star Wars*, injured Luke *needs* help. In *Forrest Gump*, Forrest *needs* to please the drill sergeant. In *Die Hard*, Hans *needs* the access code so he can get the $640 million in the vault. In *Tootsie*, Michael *needs* to tell Sandy a lie about where he got the money to do the play.

What needs are expressed in our case studies?

In *Juno*, Juno *needs* to go to the bathroom immediately.

In *The Matrix*, Neo *needs* to see what swallowing the red pill means.

In *Halloween*, Michael Myers follows Laurie and Annie (he *needs* to kill them).

In *Being John Malkovich*, Malkovich *needs* to leave for work.

In *Pulp Fiction*, Vincent *needs* to see Mia.

NOTE: Page 30 is traditionally the start of Act Two, or where the hero begins his or her Big Quest. This is also when the hero heads into a world that is a complete one-hundred-and-eighty-degree turnaround from of his normal life. That's why I call this moment the BIG QUEST ONE-EIGHTY. For example, in *The Matrix*, Neo takes the red pill, which starts him on his Big Quest to actually see what The Matrix is. His world is about to radically change, or do a One-Eighty, once he swallows that pill. Same thing happens when Craig enters the hole to see where it leads. It's leading him into John Malkovich's mind, where his world will also do a One-Eighty. In a more subtle case, Juno goes on her Big Quest to prepare for Mark and Vanessa to raise her baby, a complete One-Eighty from her normal high school way of life. Whether it's grand or small, the Big Quest One-Eighty is represented in some way.

EXERCISE THREE

For this exercise we're going to use Rob Reiner's *When Harry Met Sally* and Quentin Tarantino's *Kill Bill* to explore Minute 26's BIG UNEXPECTED. Since we're getting deeper into the movie, I'll tell you when Minute 26 starts. In *When Harry Met Sally*, Minute 26 begins when Harry and Jess (Billy Crystal and Bruno Kirby) are talking at the Giant's game, right after Harry says "I can sublet his apartment, the words are still..." Click your stopwatch on there. What's The Big Unexpected during the later part of that minute? In *Kill Bill*, Minute 26 starts when the hospital orderly tells the redneck, "Are we absolutely positively clear on rule number one?" Click your stopwatch on there and look for The Big Unexpected toward the latter part of the minute.

MINUTE 31: DISTRESS SIGNAL

Hero sees/hears something that distresses him.

Distress drops by for a visit. And since movies are sight and sound, the hero either *sees* or *hears* something that distresses him, which in turn sends out a Distress Signal to our proxy-audience. Here are a few examples:

SEEING SOMETHING DISTRESSFUL
In *Raiders of the Lost Ark*, Indy *sees* the red-hot poker moving toward Marion's face. In *Jaws*, Brody and Hooper *see* the mutilated body. In *Scream*, Sidney *sees* the mask outside and screams. In *Die Hard,* John *sees* Hans about to shoot Takagi. In *Speed*, Annie *sees* that traffic is slowing down the bomb-rigged bus. In *Rashomon*, the distressed husband *sees* the bandit coming at him with a sword.

Minute 31's Distress Signal in *Knocked Up*: Alison *tells* Ben she's pregnant, which causes him great distress.

HEARING SOMETHING DISTRESSFUL

In *Top Gun*, Maverick swallows hard when he *hears* the commander yell, "I want some butts!" In *The Sixth Sense*, Malcolm is distressed when he *hears* a potential suitor talking to Anna. In *The Godfather*, Tom *hears* the producer say that Johnny will get run out of the business, which causes him distress. In *Match Point*, Nola *tells* Chris he's going to do very well for himself unless he blows it (which causes him distress because he knows he most likely will blow it). In *Star Wars*, Ben shows distress when he hears Luke say "Obi-Wan." In *Forrest Gump*, the sergeant *yells* at Forrest, which causes him some distress.

Case studies:

In *Juno*, Juno is a bit distressed that Mark came upstairs to spy on her (SEES).

In *The Matrix*, the liquid mirror attached to Neo's fingertip causes him distress (SEES).

In *Halloween*, Laurie hears the store alarm and sees the police (HEARS & SEES).

In *Being John Malkovich*, Craig — looking through Malkovich's eyes — is distressed with what's going on (SEES).

In *Pulp Fiction*, Mia watches Vincent with the security camera — which, we find out later, causes her sexual distress (SEES).

MINUTE 32: ANXIETY AMP

Sought-after truth or object is revealed and causes great anxiety.

"Be careful what you wish for" applies during what I like to call the Anxiety Amp. During Minute 32, the revelation the hero sought after is found and amps up his (and the audience's) anxiety. Let's see how this plays out in our movie examples:

In *Die Hard*, John sees Hans shoot Takagi, which causes him great anxiety. In *Knocked Up*, Ben (who sought after Alison) experiences great anxiety over her pregnancy news. In *Spider-Man*, Osborn hears an angry voice in his head (caused from breathing the green gas he sought after). In *Raiders of the Lost Ark*, both sides want the medallion and shoot at each other for it. In *Jaws*, an anxious Hooper says, "This was no boat accident — it was a shark!"

In *The Sixth Sense*, Malcolm sees the guy who spoke with Anna, and notices that he likes her more than just a friend. In *Scream*, Deputy Dwight shows the Sergeant the mask and costume, which causes him anxiety. In *The Godfather*, the producer sees blood on his sheets, which causes him great anxiety (happens 30 seconds later in this case). In *Match Point*, Chris blows it by making a pass at Nola, which causes her anxiety. In *Star Wars*, C-3PO shows great anxiety when he discovers that his arm is ripped off. In *Forrest Gump*, Forrest discovers Jenny was thrown out of school, which causes him anxiety.

In *Tootsie*, Sandy catches Michael undressing, which causes him great anxiety. In *Speed*, the bus driver won't let Jack on the bus, which causes him great anxiety.

What's the Anxiety Amp in our case studies?

In *Juno*, Mark's comment that the nineties were the best time for rock-and-roll causes Juno anxiety.

In *Halloween*, the burglarized store causes Dr. Loomis great anxiety.

In *Being John Malkovich*, Craig falls next to the Jersey Turnpike, which causes him great anxiety.

The '50s restaurant they arrive at in *Pulp Fiction* causes Vincent anxiety — he wants to go get a steak instead.

Minute 32 in *The Matrix*: The liquid mirror Neo sought to touch creeps up his arm and into his throat. He screams! — Anxiety Amp.

MINUTE 33: OMINOUS OH NO!

Hero sees/does/hears something ominous.

The definition of the Ominous Oh No! is: *The foreshadowing of evil or tragic developments; potentially harmful or having an injurious effect.* SEEING something ominous seems to be the most popular way to relay this menacing feeling to the audience during Minute 33….

SEES

In *Raiders of the Lost Ark*, Indy sees a flame race toward his face. In *Jaws*, Brody and locals see fisherman bring in a shark. In *Knocked-Up*, Ben and Alison see a bunch of crying babies in the doctor's lobby. In *The Godfather*, the producer finds his prized horse's head in the bed. In *Match Point*, Chris stares at Nola while Tom and Chloe are dangerously close. In *Forrest Gump*, Forrest sees people laughing at Jenny.

In *Tootsie*, Michael is concerned how he looks. In *Speed*, traffic slows down Jack.

DOES

In *Spider-Man*, Peter tells his uncle not to preach at him (ominous words). In *Scream*, Sidney can't find her father.

HEARS

In *The Sixth Sense*, Cole tells his teacher, "They used to hang people here." In *Star Wars*, Luke wishes he could've met his father (which concerns Obi-Wan, who knows the truth). In *Die Hard*, John hopes Argyle heard the gunshot.

"Either obey the rules or you're history!" — Ominous words from Metcalf during Minute 33 in *Top Gun*.

How does the Ominous Oh No! show up in the case studies?

In *Juno*, Vanessa (the hero in this case) is concerned that Mark is playing music with Juno (HEARS).

In *The Matrix*, Neo sees that he's naked inside a glass pod — and so are millions of others (SEES).

In *Halloween*, Laurie doesn't notice that Michael Myers is watching her (DOES).

Looking around, Craig wonders how he's going to get back to work in *Being John Malkovich*. (SEES).

In *Pulp Fiction*, Vincent sees he won't get the food nor atmosphere he prefers (SEES).

MINUTE 34: FRIEND AFFECT

Ally's behavior affects the hero.

On Page 34 of your script, the ally does something that directly affects your hero. This is either expressed in words or deeds. I call this the Friend Affect, and this is how our movie examples apply this technique to either test or help the hero....

WORDS

In *Spider-Man*, Uncle Ben's words make Peter angry. In *Top Gun*, Goose tells Maverick he hopes they graduate. In *Little Miss Sunshine*, Frank's sarcasm pisses off Richard. In *Match Point*, Chloe's dad says they are going to move Chris up in the business. In *Star Wars*, Obi-Wan talks about the Dark Side, which affects Luke. In *Speed*, the bus driver can't hear Jack yell "there's a bomb on the bus!"

DEEDS

In *Tootsie*, Jeff fixes Michael's wig. In *Raiders of the Lost Ark*, Sallah brings Indy and Marion to his home. In *Jaws*, Quint laughs at Brody for thinking the fishermen captured the right shark. The staring teacher angers Cole in *The Sixth Sense*. In *Scream*, Billy stares at Sidney with wounded eyes. In *The Godfather*, the Turk makes heroin, which affects Don Corleone. In *Knocked Up*, the baby on the monitor freaks out Ben and Alison. In *Forrest Gump*, Jenny's pretty singing affects Forrest emotionally.

Action dominates the case studies:

In *Juno*, Mark's odd behavior affects Vanessa (ACTION).

In *The Matrix*, Morpheus's machine grabs Neo by the throat (ACTION).

In *Halloween*, the girl's parents — who Annie is babysitting for — leave for the night (ACTION).

In *Being John Malkovich*, Maxine acts like she doesn't give a damn, which affects Craig's mood (ACTION).

Minute 34 in *Pulp Fiction:* Mia takes off her jacket, revealing her attractive body to Vincent (ACTION) – Friend Affect.

MINUTE 35: BAIT & SWITCH

Seems like this new world is positive, but is it really?

The Bait & Switch affects the audience because things seem hunky-dory, peachy keen, aces up, but then there's a dark undercurrent that keeps them off balance.

In *Spider-Man*, the ringleader says they will give $3,000 to any challenger who beats the undefeated wrestler (Peter will later get screwed out of the money). In *Raiders of the Lost Ark*, Marion befriends a monkey (who will later betray her). In *Jaws*, Hooper says the fishermen may have caught the right shark (but it's a hundred-to-one it isn't). In *The Sixth Sense*, Malcolm enters for another positive session with Cole (but Cole doesn't want to talk). They're putting Billy in jail in *Scream* (but is Sidney really safe?).

Minute 35's Bait & Switch in *Little Miss Sunshine*: Richard gets a call from his agent (+), but finds out bad news (-).

In *The Godfather*, Tom thinks there's a lot of money in narcotics, which they should go after (but Don Corleone resists the idea). In *Knocked Up*, Jay thinks it's awesome that Ben's going to have a baby (but Ben is upset). In *Star Wars*, Leia's hologram pops up (but she carries bad news).

In *Die Hard*, John sees fire trucks coming to the rescue (but then they turn around). In *Tootsie*, Michael starts his new job (but finds out he has to kiss Dr. Brewster). In *Speed*, the bus driver gets the message (but he starts to slow down, which will ignite the bomb).

What's the Bait & Switch in our case studies?

In *Juno*, Vanessa is thrilled that Juno is going to give them her baby (+), but Mark isn't as thrilled (-).

In *The Matrix*, Neo is welcomed to the real world (+), but he's stuck with hundreds of acupuncture needles (-).

In *Halloween*, happy Annie walks inside with the little girl (+), not knowing Michael Myers is watching her (-).

In *Being John Malkovich*, Maxine wants to sell tickets to Malkovich's brain with Craig (+), but Lotte enters during their call (-).

Mia orders a $5 shake (+), but Vincent thinks it's too much to pay (-).

MINUTE 36: HIDE & SEEK

Main object of desire stays hidden.

This minute entices the audience with something I spoke about earlier; something that goes back to our childhood: Hide & Seek. Your friends hid and you searched for them. We desired to discover where they were hidden. Magicians manipulate this same desire in their magic tricks. They make an object or an audience member disappear. The audience waits in anticipation until he brings the object or the audience member back. Top-notch screenwriters perform the same prestidigitation during Minute 36.

Minute 36's Hide and Seek in *The Sixth Sense*: During his magic trick, Malcolm keeps the penny hidden.

Charlotte tells Maverick that she doesn't date students (she keeps her true feelings for Maverick *hidden*). In *Spider-Man*, the $3,000 Peter seeks stays *hidden* until Peter defeats the wrestler. In *Raiders of the Lost Ark*, the ark stays *hidden*, not found yet by Belloq or Indy. In *Jaws*, the evidence remains *hidden* within the shark's belly. In *Scream*, the identity of the killer remains *hidden*.

In *Little Miss Sunshine*, Richard *hides* the porn magazines from his former lover (5 seconds later in this case). In *The Godfather*, the heroin stays *hidden* until Don Corleone hands over the money. In *Knocked Up*, Alison keeps her pregnancy *hidden* from her bosses. In *Die Hard*, the bad guy looks for John, who remains *hidden*. In *Tootsie*, Dr. Brewster desires to kiss Michael, but Michael keeps his face *hidden* from him. The bomber stays *hidden* in *Speed*.

How do things remain hidden in our case studies?

In *Juno*, the baby stays *hidden* underneath Juno's bulbous belly.

In *The Matrix*, Neo's true potential remains *hidden* within his doubting mind.

In *Halloween*, Dr. Loomis searches for Michael Myers at his old house, but he's not there (he remains *hidden*).

In *Being John Malkovich*, Lotte wants to go into the portal, but it's at Craig's work (the portal remains temporarily *hidden* from her).

In *Pulp Fiction*, Vincent *hides* his attraction for Mia.

MINUTE 37: OVER HIS HEAD

Hero or ally realizes he may be in over his head.

How many times have we found ourselves in Over Our Head in life? We immediately have to flail our arms and kick our feet to reach the water's surface before we drown. So it is for our hero and audience during this minute.

A prime example of Over His Head is when Dr. Brewster kisses Michael (as "Dorothy") in *Tootsie* (Michael suddenly realizes that he may have bit off *way* more than he can chew taking this soap opera job). In *Spider-Man*, Peter suddenly realizes he's going to be involved in a cage match (he may be in over his head). In *Raiders of the Lost Ark*, Sallah realizes the ark should remain undisturbed (they may be in over their heads). In *Jaws*, Brody realizes that the woman lost her only son (he may be in over his head). In *Little Miss Sunshine*, Frank realizes that his former lover's new boyfriend is in the car (he may be in over his head emotionally).

In *The Godfather*, Sonny realizes that his father won't take the guaranteed heroin money based on principal (he may be in over his head if he oversteps his father's wishes). In *Die Hard*, John realizes that the bad guy is tougher than he thought (he may be in over his head). In *Forrest Gump*, Forrest realizes he's in a new country (he may be in over his head). In *Star Wars*, Luke realizes he must learn the ways of The Force (he may be in over his head). When Maverick opens Charlotte's note, in *Top Gun*, he realizes she wants to have dinner with him (he may be in over his head if he starts a relationship with his instructor).

How may the hero or ally be in over their head in our case studies?

In *Juno*, Juno sees the ultrasound and realizes the baby now has feet and a beating heart.

In *Halloween*, Dr. Loomis realizes he may be in over his head pursuing Michael Myers.

In *Being John Malkovich*, Lotte realizes that the portal is scarier than she thought.

In *Pulp Fiction*, Vincent realizes he's attracted to his boss's wife.

Minute 37 in *The Matrix*: Neo realizes that there is something attached to the back of his head. He may be in over his head.

MINUTE 38:
POSITIVE RECONNECT

Hero reconnects with ally(s) in a positive way.

We all need positive reinforcement from our friends. So does the hero. But the Positive Reconnect is the screenwriter's way of luring the audience into a false sense of security. Deep down we know the good times can't last. Something bad will interrupt the hero again, but we don't know exactly when, which creates anticipation.

For example, in *Top Gun*, Maverick and Goose high-five as they play volleyball. In *Raiders of the Lost Ark*, Indy and Marion joke together at the market. In *Jaws*, Brody has a touching moment with his son. In *The Sixth Sense*, Malcolm watches his wedding video.

In *The Godfather*, Johnny Fontaine sends Don Corleone flowers. In *Knocked Up*, Ben's dad tells him that he's the best thing that ever happened to him. In *Forrest Gump*, Forrest and Bubba talk positively about shrimp. In *Tootsie*, Michael chats with Julie in a positive way.

In *Match Point*, Chris and Nola kiss — Minute 38's Positive Reconnect.

What is the Positive Reconnect in our case studies?

In *Juno*, Juno and Brenda band together to argue against the ultrasound technician.

In *The Matrix*, Neo is re-introduced to Trinity, Apoc, Switch, Tank, Dozer and Mouse — his new friends.

In *Halloween*, Dr. Loomis reconnects with Sheriff Bracken.

In *Being John Malkovich*, Lotte loves being inside the portal that Craig discovered.

In *Pulp Fiction*, Vincent and Mia smile at each other.

MINUTE 39: NEW JOURNEY BOND

Hero bonds further with main ally on new journey.

In the previous minute, the hero reconnected with the ally in a positive way, but now, to keep the story moving forward, there must be a new journey that propels them into action.

In *Forrest Gump*, Forrest and Bubba bond as they get ready for their new Vietnam journey with Lt. Dan. In *Tootsie*, "Dorothy" and Julie bond on their new journey as friends. In *The Sixth Sense*, Cole repeats Malcolm's magic trick to a kid (even though Malcolm isn't there, it shows that Cole is bonding with him — they are starting a new journey of trust together). In *The Godfather*, Michael and Kate buy Christmas presents as they start their new life together.

In *Match Point*, Chris and Nola fall into the field and make love (starting a new journey of infidelity together). In *Knocked Up*, Ben and Alison talk on the phone and decide to keep the baby (they start their new journey as possible parents). In *Die Hard*, John confiscates a machine gun (his main ally in this case) for his new journey to kill the bad guys.

How does the hero bond with their ally, and what is their new journey in our case studies?

In *Juno*, Juno and Brenda laugh together as they continue on their new journey as allies.

In *The Matrix*, Neo bonds further with the Nebuchadnezzar crew as they prepare to defeat the Matrix.

In *Halloween*, Laurie reads to the boy she's babysitting, preparing him for bed.

In *Being John Malkovich*, Craig and Lotte drive together to Dr. Lester's house.

In *Pulp Fiction*, Vincent drinks Mia's shake while she looks at him with desire (they are starting a new journey as possible lovers).

MINUTE 40: ALLY'S WORLD

We learn more about the ally and their world.

During this minute, the focus is taken off the hero and we get a glimpse into the ally's world. Why? Well, since the ally is key in the hero's life, we need to let the audience know them a little better. There are a number of reasons for this: 1) Either the writer wants us to like the ally (so we approve of the hero being with them); 2) We need to fear *for* them (to understand what the hero goes through if they are put into danger); 3) We need to fear the ally (so we, in turn, fear for the hero); 4) We need to understand what the ally is capable of (which will play out later in the story); 5) We need a clearer understanding of the ally and their world (so we know what the hero is dealing with).

1) TO MAKE US LIKE THEM

In *Jaws*, Hooper loves sharks and is passionate about studying them (we almost instantly like someone who is passionate about something). In *Little Miss Sunshine*, Olive stands all alone at the gas station (we pity Olive because she's left by herself, which, in turn, makes us like her). In *Match Point*, Nola takes a call from her agent; she wants the part (we see that she's trying to pursue her dream, which makes us cheer for her a little bit more). In *Top Gun*, Charlotte keeps a cozy house and likes to make dinner (we see that she'd make a good girlfriend or wife for Maverick, which endears her to us).

Ally's World during Minute 40 in *Tootsie*: Julie signs autographs for her fans (we see she's nice to them, which makes us like her. The result? We approve of Michael pursuing her).

2) TO MAKE US FEAR FOR THEM

In *Forrest Gump*, we learn that Lt. Dan had relatives who died in every war (since it's likely that he, too, will die, it makes us cheer for him to live). In *Die Hard*, Hans threatens Holly and her coworkers (we see this so we cheer for John to save her).

3) TO MAKE US UNDERSTAND WHAT THEY ARE CAPABLE OF

In *Raiders of the Lost Ark*, we learn that Marion will hurt someone to defend herself — she clanks the guy over the head with a pan (this plays out later when she pulls a knife on Belloq).

In *Speed*, we learn that Annie had her driver's license revoked for speeding (it shows that Annie is capable of driving the bus fast).

4) TO GIVE US A CLEARER UNDERSTANDING OF THEIR WORLD

In *The Godfather*, we learn that Luca Brasi is a hitman for the family (we get a clearer understanding of what Don Corleone's world is). In *Scream*, Gale Weathers puts makeup on her black eye (we get a clearer understanding that Gale's first priority is her job and appearance).

Which one of these do our case studies use?

In *Juno*, Mark likes ginseng coolers (GIVES US A CLEARER UNDERSTANDING OF HIM AND HIS WORLD).

In *The Matrix*, Morpheus explains more about his world inside the computer program (GIVES US A CLEARER UNDER-STANDING OF HIM AND HIS WORLD).

In *Halloween*, Annie babysits across the street (TO MAKE US FEAR FOR HER).

In *Being John Malkovich*, Lotte sees that Dr. Lester has numerous pictures of Malkovich (MAKES US FEAR FOR HER).

In *Pulp Fiction*, Mia goes to the bathroom to snort cocaine (GIVES US A CLEARER UNDERSTANDING OF HER AND HER WORLD).

EXERCISE FOUR

For this exercise we're going to use Jean Pierre Jeunet's *Amélie* and James Cameron's *Titanic* to find out how the female leads, Amélie and Rose, are in OVER THEIR HEADS during Minute 37. HINT: In *Amélie*, start your stopwatch when Amélie is watching TV and the narrator says, "…with the ebb and flow of universal woe." In *Titanic*, start your stopwatch when Rose grips the railing (right after Jack looks up at the stars while lying on the bench).

 # THE HOOK OF REVELATIONS
MINUTE 41: THORNY ROSE

Things may seem kinda rosy, but there's still ugliness out there.

During this minute we feel a moment of positive relief for the hero (the rose), but then he's immediately pricked with a thorn — a problem he must solve.

For example, in *Spider-Man*, Peter feels cocky about telling off the crooked manager, but then he finds Uncle Ben shot. In *Raiders of the Lost Ark*, Indy shoots sword-guy and is temporarily safe, but he still has to find Marion. In *Jaws*, Hooper interrupts the nice dinner to tell Brody that the shark is still out there. In *Top Gun*, things are going well between Maverick and Charlotte, but she still wants to know about the MiG. The kids at the party pretend to like Cole in *The Sixth Sense*, but they really want to lock him in the closet. In *Scream*, Cotton Weary was captured, but the real killer is still out there.

Grandpa offers Richard encouraging words in *Little Miss Sunshine*, but he still doesn't have the book deal. In *Match Point*, Chris and Nola talk, but Nola wants to end the relationship. In *Knocked Up*, Martin's girlfriend smiles and says, "I heard you're pregnant," then adds: "I bet that's gonna hurt a lot." In *Star Wars*, Luke finally reaches home, but finds his aunt and uncle burned to death.

In *Forrest Gump*, Forrest likes the long walks the soldiers take, but the enemy may be close by. In *Die Hard*, John secretly listens to the bad guys' conversation, but they still hold Holly hostage. Michael likes Julie in *Tootsie*, but she's dating the asshole director. In *Speed*, the cops are on the way to help, but the bomb is still attached to the bus.

In *The Godfather*, Luca is offered a drink by the bad guys who plan to murder him — Minute 41's The Thorny Rose.

What's the Thorny Rose in our case studies?

In *Juno*, Mark composes lucrative music for commercials (the rose), but Juno calls him a sellout (the thorn).

In *The Matrix*, the world Neo lived in was nice (the rose) compared to its ugly reality (the thorn).

In *Halloween*, Laurie laughs with Annie on the phone (the rose), but the little boy interrupts and says the boogie-man is outside (the thorn).

In *Being John Malkovich*, Lotte likes that Malkovich has a portal (the rose) but is concerned as to exactly why (the thorn).

In *Pulp Fiction*, Vincent likes the restaurant now (the rose), but he doesn't think much of the waiter (the thorn).

MINUTE 42: SURPRISE REVEAL

Ally/Hero reveals something surprising.

Our ears perk up when our friends tell us something surprising, don't they? Same trick works in movie storytelling, which is used during Minute 42 to reel in the audience. Sometimes the Surprise Reveal is a negative surprise, sometimes positive, as we'll see in the following examples....

Minute 42 in *Jaws*: Hooper tells Brody that he's leaving tomorrow for a research expedition — Surprise Reveal.

NEGATIVE SURPRISE

In *Spider-Man*, Uncle Ben reveals that he's dying. In *Scream*, Gale Weathers tells Sidney that someone framed Cotton Weary. In *Knocked Up*, Alison says that she didn't want a baby for at least ten years; Ben's surprised she even had sex with him. In *Tootsie*, Michael reveals that he doesn't want Jeff to answer the phone and blow his charade.

POSITIVE SURPRISE

In *Raiders of the Lost Ark*, Marion reveals she's hiding inside the basket. In *Match Point*, Chris is surprised to see his former tennis buddy. Luke tells Obi-Wan that he wants to become a Jedi. In *Speed*, the bus driver tells Jack there's an access panel that leads under the bus.

And what surprising revelation is made in our case studies?

In *Juno*, Juno surprises Mark with the ultrasound picture (NEGATIVE SURPRISE).

In *The Matrix*, Morpheus reveals that humans are used as batteries (NEGATIVE SURPRISE).

In *Halloween*, the dog barks when he sees Michael Myers (NEGATIVE SURPRISE).

In *Being John Malkovich*, Lotte surprises Craig at work, wanting to go into the portal again (NEGATIVE SURPRISE).

In *Pulp Fiction*, Vincent surprises Mia by bringing up the story about the guy who was thrown out the window (NEGATIVE SURPRISE).

MINUTE 43: SURPRISE REVEAL 2

Ally reveals something even more surprising.

What if your friend, who just revealed something surprising to you, followed up with something even *more* surprising? We'd be riveted and want to know more. So will the audience. Death, or the mention of possible death, seems to be a popular Surprise Reveal during Minute 46.

DEATH SURPRISE

In *Raiders of the Lost Ark*, Marion dies! In *Spider-Man*, Uncle Ben is dying. In *Top Gun*, Maverick reveals that it's a mystery how his dad died. In *Jaws*, Hooper reveals that sharks attack people in three feet of water. In *The Godfather*, the betrayer stabs Luca through the hand. In *Star Wars*, Obi-Wan tells Luke (about Mos Eisley Spaceport), "You will never find a more wretched hive of scum and villainy. We must be cautious" (they may die there). In *Speed*, Annie tells Jack that traffic has stopped up ahead! (They could crash and die). In *Die Hard*, Holly reveals to Harry that John is their only hope for survival.

OTHER SURPRISES

In *The Sixth Sense*, the doctor reveals that he thinks Cole's mom beats her son. In *Scream*, Billy surprises Sidney when she turns the corner. In *Little Miss Sunshine*, Richard says, "What a fuckin' nightmare" (a surprising swear word for the straight-laced Richard to use). In *Forrest Gump*, a surprisingly strong rain arrives and keeps coming.

Much to Alison's surprise in *Knocked Up*, Ben reveals that he's going to read the baby books — Minute 43's Surprise Reveal 2.

And what do our case studies reveal that's even more surprising?

In *Juno*, Mark reveals that he loves really gruesome horror movies.

In *The Matrix*, Morpheus reveals that there are human crops used for harvesting.

In *Halloween*, the boy says that the boogie-man is after him.

In *Being John Malkovich*, Lotte reveals that she's a transsexual.

In *Pulp Fiction*, Mia reveals that the guy didn't get thrown out of the window for massaging her feet.

MINUTE 44: NEW NEWS

Hero reacts to new news.

During this minute the hero either reacts to the last minute's surprise, or reacts to New News, which is often surprising.

HERO REACTS TO WHAT HAPPENED IN THE PREVIOUS MINUTE
Enraged that his Uncle Ben isn't coming back to life, Peter hunts down Uncle Ben's murderer to seek revenge in *Spider-Man*.

But mostly, the hero **REACTS TO NEW NEWS**
For example, in *Jaws*, Brody becomes deeply disappointed when Hooper doesn't find the girl inside the shark. In *The Sixth Sense* Cole says to Malcolm, "Tell me a story about why you're sad." Malcolm grows serious and says, "You think I'm sad?" (He reacts badly to the news that Cole can tell he's upset). In *Scream*, Sidney reacts when Billy says he wants his girlfriend back.

In *The Godfather*, Don Corleone reacts when he sees two armed men approaching him. In *Little Miss Sunshine*, Dwayne reacts when he hears his parents arguing. In *Match Point*, Chris reacts when Eleanor asks him and Chloe when they are going to get married. In *Knocked Up*, Pete (the hero in this case) reacts badly when Debbie says they'll help raise the baby.

New News during Minute 44 in *Raiders of the Lost Ark*: Reacting to Marion's death in the previous minute, Indy gets drunk.

In *Star Wars*, Luke reacts when Ben uses The Force on the Stormtroopers. In *Forrest Gump*, Forrest reacts favorably to Bubba's offer to start a shrimping business with him. In *Die Hard*, John yells at police dispatch for not taking his call seriously. In *Tootsie*, Michael reacts to getting asked for an autograph. When he sees the red light in *Speed*, Jack yells at Annie to keep going.

What news does the hero react to in our case studies?

In *Juno*, Juno is impressed that Mark's taste in horror movies is excellent.

In *The Matrix*, Neo throws up after experiencing all this overwhelming new information.

In *Halloween*, Annie reacts when the light switch doesn't work.

In *Being John Malkovich*, Craig reacts to Lotte's transsexuality news.

In *Pulp Fiction*, Vincent smiles at Mia's new information about the so-called massage incident.

MINUTE 45:
OUT OF THE ORDINARY

Hero does something brave and out of the ordinary for him.

This is the minute we see another side of the hero — something Out Of The Ordinary. It's a moment when the hero shows courage. This moment makes us respect the hero on a subconscious level because we admire people who show this quality. Why? Because stepping out of your comfort zone is extremely difficult to do. If they can do it, maybe the audience can too.

Here are a few examples of the hero's bravery: In *Star Wars*, Luke enters the dangerous cantina with Obi-Wan. In *Die Hard*, John leaps off a ledge (even though he's scared of heights). In *Raiders of the Lost Ark*, Indy threatens to kill Belloq in a public place. In *Top Gun*, Maverick flirts with Charlotte at work. In *The Sixth Sense*, Malcolm tells Cole why he's sad. In *Scream*, sweet Sidney yells at her boyfriend for being selfish. Peter viciously pummels the bad guy in *Spider-Man*.

In *Little Miss Sunshine*, even though it's hard for her, Olive tells Grandpa that she doesn't want to be a loser. Bachelor Chris marries Chloe in *Match Point*. In *Knocked Up*, Ben agrees to take it slower with Alison.

Minute 45 in *Jaws*: Even though he's afraid of water and boats, Brody heads out to sea with Hooper — Out Of The Ordinary.

And what do our case study heroes do that's brave and out-of-the-ordinary for them?

In *Juno*, Juno flirts with married Mark.

In *The Matrix*, Neo has his mind freed at an older-than-usual age.

Despite Michael Myers being outside, Annie leaves the door open as she does the laundry in *Halloween*.

In *Being John Malkovich*, Maxine (the hero in this case) calls Malkovich and asks him on a date.

In *Pulp Fiction*, reserved Vincent agrees to enter a dance contest.

MINUTE 46: THE REVELATION

Revelations, doled out bit by bit, are like clues left on a trail leading somewhere interesting for the audience. The Revelation comes in four different forms during Minute 46: 1) Revelations that rock the hero's world; 2) Revelations about the ally; 3) Revelations about the hero; 4) Revelations about the bad guy.

REVELATIONS THAT ROCK THE HERO'S WORLD

In *Spider-Man*, Uncle Ben's killer is the thief who Peter let go earlier! In *Forrest Gump*, the enemy shoots at Forrest and his platoon, revealing they are in the area. In *Speed*, Annie reveals to Jack that they are going the wrong way.

REVELATION ABOUT THE ALLY

In *Raiders of the Lost Ark*, Sallah reveals that he is willing to risk his children to save Indy. In *Jaws*, Hooper reveals that his family is rich. In *Top Gun*, Charlotte stares at Maverick for a long time, revealing her growing feelings. In *Star Wars*, the bartender reveals his prejudice by telling Luke (concerning the droids), "we don't serve their kind here."

REVELATION ABOUT THE HERO

In *The Sixth Sense*, Malcolm reveals to Cole that his wife doesn't like the person he has become. In *Scream*, classmates reveal that they think Sidney committed the murder and that "her mother was a tramp." In *Knocked Up*, Alison reveals to her nieces that Ben is her "boyfriend."

REVELATION ABOUT THE BAD GUY

In *Tootsie*, the director reveals that he's having an affair with another actress.

The Revelation during Minute 46 in *The Godfather*: Kate shows Michael the newspaper article about his father being shot.

And what type of revelation is made in our case studies?

In *Juno*, Juno reveals that she and Brenda were escorted off the hospital premises (REVELATION ABOUT THE HERO AND ALLY).

In *The Matrix*, Morpheus reveals that he believes Neo will lead humanity to freedom (REVELATION ABOUT THE HERO).

In *Halloween*, Annie can't hear the girl calling for her (REVELATION ABOUT THE ALLY).

In *Being John Malkovich*, Lotte reveals that she wants to meet with Maxine as Malkovich (REVELATION ABOUT THE ALLY).

In *Pulp Fiction*, Vincent reveals that he can dance pretty well (REVELATION ABOUT THE HERO).

MINUTE 47: THE ESCORT

Ally takes, or will take, the hero somewhere.

One of the functions of the ally, especially during Minute 47, is to lead the hero somewhere. This action drives the hero, and the story, forward to fresh territories.

In *Jaws*, Hooper *takes* Brody out into the ocean at night. In *Raiders of the Lost Ark*, Sallah says he will *take* Indy to the old man. The moped (the ally in this case) *takes* Richard down the road in *Little Miss Sunshine*. In *The Godfather*, Kate *takes* Michael home to his father. In *Match Point*, Tom *takes* Chris toward the bench to talk.

In *Knocked Up*, the nieces *take* Ben to the backyard. In *Star Wars*, Obi-Wan *takes* Luke away from the fight. In *Tootsie*, Julie will *take* Michael to her apartment to rehearse. In *Speed*, Annie drives the bus to the empty road (which *takes* Jack to a safer place).

Where do the allies take the hero in our case studies?

In *Juno*, Mark *escorts* Juno to the front door and opens it for her.

In *The Matrix*, Tank says he will *take* Neo to his training.

In *Halloween*, the girl *leads* Annie toward the house.

In *Being John Malkovich*, Malkovich *takes* Lotte (in his mind) to the restaurant.

In *Pulp Fiction*, Mia *takes* Vincent deeper into their relationship.

MINUTE 48: NEEDED KNOWLEDGE

Ally gives/shows hero needed knowledge.

The next three minutes are devoted to giving the hero knowledge. The knowledge the ally gives the hero (and the audience) during Minute 48 aids the hero's goal or situation, or shows him what he needs to do next. You'll also notice that during these three minutes the knowledge becomes more and more ominous as the minutes progress....

KNOWLEDGE AIDS THE HERO'S GOAL OR SITUATION

In *Raiders of the Lost Ark,* Sallah tells Indy the Nazis had a headpiece. In *Spider-Man,* Harry tells Peter that his father got the place in New York, so they're all set for the fall. In *Jaws,* Hooper shows Brody that Ben Gardner's boat is torn up.

In *Top Gun,* Charlotte tells Maverick that his encounter was a victory, but was an example of what not to do. In *The Sixth Sense,* Cole tells Malcolm he sees dead people all the time. In *Little Miss Sunshine,* the hotel sign (his ally in this case) shows Richard where his agent is. In *Star Wars,* Han tells Obi-Wan and Luke that his spaceship is fast.

KNOWLEDGE SHOWS THE HERO WHAT HE NEEDS TO DO NEXT

In *The Godfather,* the ally tells Sonny that the bodyguard is sick. In *Match Point,* the maintenance man tells Chris that Nola moved out. In *Knocked Up,* Debbie tells Alison that Ben is overweight and has bad genes. In *Die Hard,* the small open door (John's ally in this case) shows John the knowledge he needs to escape.

What knowledge is given to the hero in our case studies?

In *Juno,* Brenda tells Juno that she can't just "drop in" on Mark and Vanessa.

In *Halloween*, Paul tells horny Annie he wants to come over and have sex with her.

In *Being John Malkovich*, Lotte tells Malkovich that she likes Maxine.

In *Pulp Fiction*, Mia gives Vincent a flirtatious look, suggesting she wants him.

Minute 48 in *The Matrix*: Tank inputs combat knowledge directly into Neo's brain — Needed Knowledge.

MINUTE 49: FOREBODING FACT

Hero is given more knowledge/warning, often ominous.

A dark undertone accompanies the knowledge during Minute 49, which is why this minute is called Foreboding Fact.

For example, in *Top Gun*, Charlotte explains how a textbook maneuver should be executed (if Maverick doesn't do it this way he might die). In *Jaws*, as Hooper climbs into the ominous water, he tells Brody, "I'll be back in two minutes" (he hopes). In *Scream* (13 seconds later in this case), the principal warns the students that there's a citywide curfew because of the murders.

Minute 49 in *Raiders of the Lost Ark*: The old man cautions Indy that the medallion warns against disturbing the ark — the Foreboding Fact.

In *Tootsie*, Michael finds out Julie has a son. In *Little Miss Sunshine*, the agent tells Richard, "It's not the program, it's *you*." In *The Godfather*, Tom is mistakenly told that Don Corleone is dead. In *Match Point*, Chloe tells Chris that they haven't made love in a week. In *Knocked Up*, Pete tells Ben that happy kids reveal how inadequate they are as adults.

In *Star Wars*, Han wants an overpriced "ten thousand" to fly Luke and Obi-Wan to Alderaan. In *Forrest Gump*, Forrest discovers that Lt. Dan is wounded. In *Die Hard*, John sees that the shaft is dangerously deep. In *Speed*, the Captain tells Jack that there's a hard turn ahead.

What's the Foreboding Fact in the case studies?

In *Juno*, Brenda tells Juno to "go fly a kite" (she's not pleased with Juno's smart-ass attitude, a Foreboding Fact in their mother/step-daughter relationship).

In *The Matrix*, Tank gives Neo deadly fighting knowledge (if he doesn't have this knowledge he will die in The Matrix).

In *Halloween*, Michael Myers appears, giving the audience (the hero in this case) the Foreboding Fact that he is watching Annie go to Laurie's house.

In *Being John Malkovich*, Craig lies to Lotte, saying he can't invite Maxine to dinner because there's tension between them (Craig is willing to lie to Lotte – a Foreboding Fact for the audience).

In *Pulp Fiction*, Vincent warns himself in the mirror not to have sex with Mia (if he does, Marselles will probably kill him).

MINUTE 50: THE PORTENT

Something potentially deadly is seen or explained.

The knowledge given during Minute 50 is laced with death, either: Actual Death, Death of a Dream, or Death of a Relationship. This is why this minute is called The Portent, which means: *An indication that something calamitous may occur.*

ACTUAL DEATH

In *Raiders of the Lost Ark*, Sallah spots the dead monkey and catches the poisoned date before Indy eats it. In *Jaws*, Hooper finds a shark's tooth in the ship's hull and sees a human head. In *The Sixth Sense*, Cole's mom discovers rips in Cole's clothing and gashes on his back. In *Scream*, Gale tells Dewey, "We got a serial killer on our hands." In *The Godfather*, Tom tells his former ally that "Sonny will come after him with everything he's got" (meaning, Sonny is going to kill his enemy). In *Star Wars*, weapon-carrying Stormtroopers look for Obi-Wan and Luke; Greedo wants Jabba's money from Han (or they will kill him). In *Forrest Gump*, the enemy shoots Forrest. In *Speed*, the Captain tells another officer, "We have a window, I wanna make sure it stays open!" (potentially deadly to Jack if they don't take advantage). In *Die Hard*, the strap (John's ally in this case) starts slipping, which could be deadly to John.

DEATH OF A DREAM

In *Little Miss Sunshine*, the agent tells Richard that it's time to move on (death of his dream). In *Top Gun*, Charlotte, Maverick's instructor, confesses that she's fallen for him (could be the death of her dream job). In *Tootsie*, Julie asks "Dorothy" if she's ever concerned about wearing so much makeup (could be the death of Michael's charade, and possibly his job).

DEATH OF A RELATIONSHIP

In *Knocked Up*, the guys tell Ben that they can't launch the website until it's ready, but Ben needs the money now (or it could be the death of his and Alison's relationship).

What is The Portent in our case studies?

In *Juno*, Juno tells us — through narration — about Paulie's mom, who doesn't like her (deadly to her and Paulie's relationship).

In *The Matrix*, Morpheus tells Neo, "Your weakness is not your technique" (if Neo doesn't overcome his weakness he will die).

In *Halloween*, the TV forewarns of impending doom: "And now, the horrifying conclusion...."

In *Being John Malkovich*, Maxine tells a potential client that they can go inside Malkovich's brain for $200 (a potentially dangerous proposition for the client).

In *Pulp Fiction*, Mia finds Vincent's highly potent heroin.

EXERCISE FIVE

We're going to explore Minute 41's THE ROSY THORN in this exercise. In Jason Reitman's *Up In The Air*, Ryan (George Clooney) is in the lobby, content to start another workday, when he overhears Natalie say something to her boyfriend on the cell phone. What does she say that sticks a thorn into his rosy thoughts about himself? (This happens just after they enter the near-empty office to fire people). In David Fincher's *The Game*, Nicholas (Michael Douglas) and the waitress see an open elevator (the Rose) — a possible way out of the parking garage after being abandoned in the ambulance. What's the thorn once they're in the elevator?

MINUTE 51: THE ENGAGE

Hero and/or ally engage the enemy, the enemy intimidates the hero.

Now that the hero has his knowledge, or has been warned, the enemy shows up — I call it The Engage. It's where they mix it up for a bit, like fighters in a ring feeling each other out, testing each other's endurance for the remaining rounds. And the enemy shows up for the next three minutes. The enemy can appear in a variety of ways:

The Engage during Minute 51 in *Jaws*: Brody and Hooper tell the mayor (the enemy) about Ben Gardner's boat, but the mayor demands to see the shark's tooth.

AS A PERSON

In *Raiders of the Lost Ark*, the Nazis yell at Indy. In *Scream*, Sidney and Tatum chat with Stuart (one of the killers), and he talks them into coming to his party. In *The Godfather*, Tom listens to the betrayer (the enemy) who intimidates him into possibly helping him. In *Knocked Up*, Ben and Alison go to the gynecologist, who intimidates Alison with his attitude (the enemy). In *Star Wars*, Han shoots Greedo, which draws the attention of the other bad guys. In *Forrest Gump*, Forrest and Bubba hear the enemy coming.

AS FEELINGS

In *Top Gun*, Maverick and Charlotte engage in what they have been intimidated by all along: Their feelings of love (the enemy because of their work situation).

AS A GHOST
In *The Sixth Sense*, a dark shadow (the enemy) passes behind Cole.

AS CONSCIENCE
In *Spider-Man*, Peter and Aunt May talk about the last thing Peter said to his uncle. (Peter's conscience is the enemy, which intimidates Peter).

AS DEATH
In *Little Miss Sunshine*, the family finds out "Grandpa won't wake up."

AS WORK
In *Match Point*, claustrophobia overcomes Chris at work (his enemy in this case).

AS A TIGHT SPACE
In *Die Hard*, John crawls through the airshaft; its narrowness intimidates him.

AS A BOMB
In *Speed*, Jack and Annie keep the bus over 50 MPH so it doesn't blow up.

The possibilities are limitless. Just make sure the enemy shows up in some form during this minute. How does the enemy intimidate our case studies?

In *Juno*, Juno and Paulie talk about her pregnancy, the baby (the enemy in this case) intimidates them.

In *The Matrix*, Morpheus (who's the faux-enemy in the training exercise) intimidates Neo with his superior fighting skills.

In *Halloween*, Annie discovers that the door is locked (Michael Myers locked it from the inside), she must return to get the key.

In *Being John Malkovich*, Craig and Maxine send the client (the enemy in this case) into the Malkovich portal and he is overwhelmed by the experience.

In *Pulp Fiction*, Mia spreads out the heroin (the enemy), on which she will soon overdose on.

MINUTE 52: SAY UNCLE

When I was a kid, bullies would seize weaker classmates, put them into headlocks and force them to say "Uncle" before releasing them. The phrase originated from the similar Irish-sounding word "anacol," which means "mercy." The experience was always humiliating for the victim. That's why the phrase is fitting for Minute 52. Not only does the enemy intimidate the hero in the previous minute, now he almost defeats him, which draws even more sympathy from the audience.

For example, in *Raiders of the Lost Ark*, Nazis take Sallah away from the well opening, leaving Indy stuck inside. Despite Brody's urging in *Jaws*, the Mayor won't budge — he'll keep the beaches open. In *Top Gun*, a pilot informs Maverick that Iceman "won another one." The killer spooks the principal in *Scream*. In *Spider-Man*, Peter's guilt (the enemy in this case) almost overcomes him.

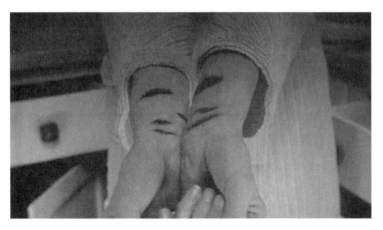

Minute 52 in *The Sixth Sense*: An angry ghost yells at Cole and shows him her slashed wrists. Cole runs for safety — Say Uncle.

In *Little Miss Sunshine*, Grandpa's serious condition almost overwhelms Sheryl. In *The Godfather*, the assassins almost kill Don Corleone. In *Match Point*, Chris leaves work (his enemy) in a panic. In *Knocked Up*, Ben's friends (enemies in this case) want him to play paintball, but Ben resists the temptation and stays with Alison instead.

In *Star Wars*, R2-D2 and C-3PO hide from the Stormtroopers. In *Forrest Gump*, a bomb almost kills Forrest. In *Die Hard*, the bad guy almost finds John in the airshaft. In *Tootsie*, Julie tells "Dorothy" to mind her own business about her drinking. In *Speed*, the officers can't access the files they need.

How does the enemy almost overcome the hero in our case studies?

In *Juno*, Juno's pregnancy (the enemy) hurts her and Paulie's chances at being a real couple.

In *The Matrix*, Morpheus (the enemy in the dojo) beats Neo in the fight.

In *Halloween*, Michael Myers chokes Annie in the car.

In *Being John Malkovich*, Maxine (the enemy) flirts with Craig's wife instead of him.

In *Pulp Fiction*, Mia overdoses on the heroin.

MINUTE 53: THE INTIMIDATION

Enemy intimidates hero.

In the Bible story of David and Goliath, the Philistine's nine-foot-tall super-soldier stood on the opposing hillside and hurled taunts at the much smaller Israelite soldiers. He did this to intimidate them, to show them who's boss. The bad guy uses this same intimidation against the hero during Minute 53. And sometimes the bad guy is simply life itself. Either way, some sort of intimidation occurs here.

In *Jaws*, the mayor tells Brody they will open the beaches on July 4th. In *Raiders of the Lost Ark*, Nazis keep Sallah away from the well hole — Indy can't get out. In *Top Gun*, Maverick discovers that Metcalf (superb flying enemy in this case) is one of the pilots. In *The Sixth Sense*, the actor kid (one of Cole's enemies) intimidates Cole because he was in a commercial. The killer stabs the principal in *Scream*.

In *Match Point*, Chloe (the enemy in this case) prevents Chris from getting to Nola at the museum. In *Knocked Up*, the costume designer notices that Alison is pregnant. In *Little Miss Sunshine*, the doctor tells the family that Grandpa is dead. In *Star Wars*, Jabba wants his money from Han. In *Forrest Gump*, the enemy's bullets kill Bubba. In *Die Hard*, John sees a big spot of blood. In *Tootsie*, Julie intimidates Michael. In *Speed*, the bomber can see — on his monitor — if Jack disobeys him.

Minute 53 in *Being John Malkovich*: Craig is stunned to silence after Maxine slaps him — The Intimidation.

What's The Intimidation in our case studies?

In *Juno*, Vanessa's desire to paint the baby's room intimidates reluctant Mark.

In *The Matrix*, Morpheus (Neo's enemy in the dojo) tells Neo to *know* he is faster.

In *Halloween*, Michael Myers kills Annie.

In *Pulp Fiction*, overdosing Mia freaks Vincent out.

MINUTE 54: THE LIGHTBULB

New positive or negative revelation is made.

Another revelation is made during this minute — a lightbulb blinks on in the mind. And the lightbulb will either illuminate something positive or negative. Whichever one it is, you must reveal something here to keep the audience interested in your story.

LIGHTBULB ILLUMINATES SOMETHING POSITIVE
In *Raiders of the Lost Ark*, Indy discovers that the sun's rays really do work through the medallion. In *Star Wars*, Han learns that Jabba will give him more time to pay his debt. In *Forrest Gump*, Forrest discovers that Lt. Dan is in the next hospital bed. In *Die Hard*, John sees that a cop car has arrived. In *Speed*, the bomber says it's okay to unload the driver.

LIGHTBULB ILLUMINATES SOMETHING NEGATIVE
In *Spider-Man*, Peter realizes that Jameson has published negative Spider-Man articles. In *Jaws*, Hooper and Brody can't find anyone to help them (they realize they are in this alone). In *Top Gun*, Maverick realizes his ego is too big to resist — he leaves his wingman to pursue Metcalf. In *The Sixth Sense*, Cole sees dead people hanging in the school hall. In *Scream*, we learn that someone is secretly watching Sidney and Tatum. In *The Godfather*, Tom learns that Sonny wants Pauly killed. In *Knocked Up*, Debbie discovers that there are sex offenders living all around them.

Minute 54 in *Little Miss Sunshine*: The administrator tells Richard he needs burial transit papers, a negative lightbulb.

What is The Lightbulb in our case studies?

In *Juno*, Juno sees Vanessa at the mall, and realizes Vanessa would be a great mom (+).

In *The Matrix*, Neo realizes he can't jump from one building to the next (-).

In *Halloween*, the boy sees Michael Myers carrying a body toward the neighbor's house (-).

In *Being John Malkovich*, Craig finds out that Maxine is attracted to Lotte (-).

In *Pulp Fiction*, Lance finds out Vincent is bringing dying Mia to his house (-).

MINUTE 55: SIDESWIPE

It's time to give the hero, and the audience, another jolt. When I was sixteen, I pulled my car onto Pennsylvania's Route 22 and a silver van sideswiped my Nova at a speed of 60 MPH. The moment seized my attention, to say the least. Movies use this same sideswipe moment to elevate our adrenaline levels and keep us glued to the screen.

In *Speed*, the bus slams into the flatbed truck (SIDESWIPE). In *Top Gun*, Jester surprises Maverick with an unexpected attack (SIDESWIPE). In *Die Hard*, a bad guy surprises John with a gun (SIDESWIPE). In *The Godfather*, the family is stunned to learn that Luca Brasi is dead (SIDESWIPE). In *Raiders of the Lost Ark*, Sallah drops the Nazi flag onto a surprised Indy (SIDESWIPE).

In *The Sixth Sense*, Cole asks Malcolm if he's ever felt the pricklies on the back of his neck. "That's them," Cole says (*sideswiping* information for Malcolm). Stormtroopers fire at Han (SIDESWIPE). Forrest gets Jenny's letters back unopened (SIDESWIPE).

What's the Sideswipe in our case studies?

In *Juno*, Juno runs into Vanessa by surprise (SIDESWIPE).

In *The Matrix*, Neo's failed jump stuns Mouse (SIDESWIPE).

In *Halloween*, Sheriff Bracken surprises Dr. Loomis (SIDESWIPE).

In *Being John Malkovich*, Malkovich kisses Maxine (SIDESWIPE).

In *Pulp Fiction*, Vincent crashes his car into Lance's house (SIDESWIPE).

NOTE: Somewhere between Minutes 55 and 62, we have what I call the MASSIVE MIDPOINT MOMENT. It's when things get way more serious for the hero, like when the creature explodes out of the crew member's chest in Ridley Scott's

Alien (55), or when Tarkin blows up Alderaan in *Star Wars* (60), or when Craig attacks Lotte with a gun in *Being John Malkovich* (60), or the bad guys blast away at Sgt. Al's police cruiser in *Die Hard* (58), or when Richard and Sheryl illegally carry Grandpa's body from the hospital in *Little Miss Sunshine* (58). The Massive Midpoint Moment is a radical event that forces the hero into seeing things through to the bitter end, whether he wants to or not. In other words, the mineshaft has collapsed behind him and the air is running out. The hero must press forward into even more dangerous territory if he hopes to ultimately reach his goal. He has to either *do* from this point on, or *die* trying (literally or figuratively).

MINUTE 56: DARK TWIST CHAT

Hero talks with a friend, and then there's a dark twist.

We're having a pleasant chat with a friend outside a grocery store. We're about to wrap up the conversation and finish our errands when they say, "Oh, did you hear that your brother-in-law was arrested?" That's the Dark Twist Chat. Suddenly we forget about our errands. We want to know more. The writer uses this same technique to make the audience forget about the outside world and keep their attention focused on the movie....

In *Spider-Man*, Peter asks out Mary Jane, but then she says, "Don't tell Harry." In *Raiders of the Lost Ark*, Indy is excited to find Marion, but then he re-gags her. In *Jaws*, the mayor (the board's hero) chats with a friend, but then he asks him to swim in the life-threatening water. In *The Sixth Sense*, Cole confides to Malcolm, "Please make them [the dead people] leave." In *Scream*, Randy chats with Stuart — he thinks Billy is the killer.

In *The Godfather*, a family member chats with a friend, but they're preparing to kill him. In *Match Point*, Chris whispers to Nola and asks for her phone number (while his wife is nearby).

In *Knocked Up*, Alison and Debbie chat about the baby crib, but then Ben suggests that they use the discarded one in the alley behind his house. In *Star Wars*, Han talks with Chewbacca while Imperial Troopers chase them.

In *Forrest Gump*, Lt. Dan talks with Forrest, but he's angry about something. In *Die Hard*, the cop wishes the receptionist a Merry Christmas, but the receptionist is a bad guy. "Dorothy" tells the director the script lines are "horseshit" in *Tootsie*. In *Speed*, Annie urges Helen not to get off the bus. She disobeys, and a small bomb kills her.

What's the Dark Twist Chat in the case studies?

The Minute 56 Dark Twist Chat in *Juno*: Juno talks Vanessa into feeling her stomach, but the baby won't kick for her.

In *The Matrix*, Trinity brings food to Neo, but then Cypher expresses jealousy.

In *Halloween*, Dr. Loomis tells Sheriff Bracken, "Death has come to your town."

In *Being John Malkovich*, Malkovich has a friendly chat with Maxine, but then Lotte enters into him and turns Maxine on.

In *Pulp Fiction*, Lance tells Vincent that he never gave an adrenaline shot before.

MINUTE 57: DIFFICULT WORDS

Difficult question/request/statement is asked/made.

The posing of a difficult question, request, or statement within a scene keeps us turning pages. Why? Because a difficult question, request, or statement *has* to be dealt with in some way. And "dealing with it" drives the story forward. For example, my friend's parents once gathered him and his sisters into the den one night. Once everyone was settled, his dad announced that he and their mom were getting a divorce. These Difficult Words caused immediate emotional upheaval within the siblings. Storytellers borrow the tension created in such moments to spark life into their movie minutes.

A few examples:
In *Scream*, Billy asks Randy, "How do we know you're not the killer?" In *Top Gun*, Iceman asks Maverick, "Whose side are you on?" "You got something you want to confess?" Mom asks Cole in *The Sixth Sense*. In *Jaws*, Brody asks his son to go to the pond (his son thinks the pond is for sissies). "You cheated me out of my destiny!" Lt. Dan tells Forrest in *Forrest Gump*. In *Speed*, the TV newscaster states that one of the passengers was killed.

During Minute 57 in *Knocked Up*: Alison's friends ask how she got pregnant — Difficult Words.

What Difficult Words made their way into our case studies?

"Can you hear me?" Vanessa asks Juno's unresponsive baby in *Juno*.

"Were you listening to me or looking at the woman in the red dress?" Morpheus asks Neo in *The Matrix*.

In *Halloween*, Sheriff Bracken says to Dr. Loomis, "Damn you for letting him go."

In *Being John Malkovich*, Maxine asks Malkovich if he minds if she calls him "Lotte."

In *Pulp Fiction*, Vincent and Lance argue over who will give Mia the adrenaline shot.

MINUTE 58: VITAL EVENT

The Vital Event is just like it sounds, and it can be portrayed in a number of ways: Something alters the hero's life; it touches upon the past; information is explained; it reveals the state of a relationship; or it poses a threat.

SOMETHING ALTERS THE HERO'S LIFE
In *Spider-Man*, Peter sees the newspaper request for Spider-Man photos. In *Knocked Up*, the guys find out that there's already a mrskin.com — their website is screwed! TV and magazines request interviews with Michael (as "Dorothy") in *Tootsie*. In *Little Miss Sunshine*, Richard and Sheryl illegally carry the body from the hospital. In *Raiders of the Lost Ark*, Major Toht shows the medallion impression burned into his palm.

IT TOUCHES UPON THE PAST
In *Top Gun*, Maverick stares at his dead father's picture.

SIGNIFICANT INFORMATION IS EXPLAINED
In *The Sixth Sense*, Cole tells his mom, "Sometimes people lose things. And they really didn't lose them, it just gets moved."

Minute 58 in *Die Hard*: Sgt. Al calls dispatch for immediate help after the bad guys blast away at his cruiser — Vital Event.

In *Star Wars*, Tarkin says he will blow up Alderaan. In *Forrest Gump*, Forrest tells Lt. Dan he's "still Lt. Dan."

IT REVEALS THE STATE OF A RELATIONSHIP

In *The Godfather*, Michael can't tell Kate, over the phone, that he loves her. In *Match Point*, Chris and his wife barely speak over breakfast. In *Speed*, the passengers start to argue. In *Scream*, Billy threatens Randy.

Minute 58 in *Rashomon*: The husband kills himself with his wife's knife — Vital Event.

IT POSES A THREAT

In *Jaws*, the little brother follows his big brother toward the dreaded water.

What's the Vital Event in our case studies?

In *Juno*, Juno calls Mark to chat about music (this is significant because they're overstepping the bounds of their relationship).

In *The Matrix*, Morpheus tells Neo that when he's ready he won't need to dodge bullets (vital information for Neo).

In *Halloween*, Lynda and her boyfriend make out, not knowing that Michael Myers is nearby.

In *Being John Malkovich*, Craig and Lotte argue over her infidelity.

In *Pulp Fiction*, Vincent stabs Mia in the heart with the adrenaline needle.

MINUTE 59: THE DECEPTION

Robert Southey once wrote that deception is "a lie reduced to practice." When we witness someone deceiving another person in real life, it creates immediate suspicion within us. Again, it goes back to self-preservation: If he deceives her, will he also deceive me? Deception can threaten our relationships, our jobs, and, ultimately, our security. But deception isn't entirely bad in some cases. When the hero uses deception to "put one over" on the bad guy, we admire his cleverness. Here are a number of ways characters deceive each other in movies:

TO FURTHER A CAREER

In *Spider-Man*, Peter snaps photos of himself as Spider-Man and sells them to Jameson. In *Tootsie*, Michael continues to pretend that he's "Dorothy" so he can keep acting.

TO AVOID GETTING CAUGHT

In *Little Miss Sunshine*, the family hides the fact that they are smuggling a body. In *Match Point*, Chris has an affair with Nola behind Chloe's back. In *Star Wars*, Tarkin deceives Leia into thinking he won't blow up Alderaan if she tells him the rebel base's location. In *Die Hard*, John doesn't tell Hans where or who he is.

The Deception during Minute 59 in *Raiders of the Lost Ark*: Indy and the workers dig at nightfall to avoid detection.

TO EASE CONCERNS
In *Jaws*, the mayor tells the news camera that the shark has been caught (he deceives the public). Unbeknownst to Michael in *The Godfather*, Sonny is going to send men to look after him.

TO ADVANCE A RELATIONSHIP
In *Top Gun*, Goose's wife secretly tells Charlotte that Maverick's in love with her. In *Knocked Up*, Ben shows Alison an engagement box — but it's empty.

TO CAUSE PROBLEMS
In *The Sixth Sense*, a ghost moves the pendant to deceive Cole's mom.

TO AVOID GETTING CAUGHT seems to be the unanimous vote for our case studies:

In *Juno*, Juno and Mark keep their feelings secret (TO AVOID GETTING CAUGHT).

In *The Matrix*, Morpheus tells the crew to set down the ship (to deceive the Sentinels) (TO AVOID GETTING CAUGHT).

In *Halloween*, Michael Myers secretly watches the couple making out (TO AVOID GETTING CAUGHT).

In *Being John Malkovich*, Craig hides under the bed and waits for Lotte (TO AVOID GETTING CAUGHT).

In *Pulp Fiction*, Vincent asks Mia not to tell Marsellus about her overdose (TO AVOID GETTING CAUGHT).

MINUTE 60: THE SHOCKER

During the one-hour mark, we experience The Shocker: Something that draws a swift inhalation of breath from the audience. And it either happens to the hero or his allies....

In *Star Wars*, Tarkin blows up Alderaan. In *Little Miss Sunshine*, the family stuffs Grandpa's dead body into the van and drives off. In *Scream*, the Chief tells Dewey that tomorrow is the anniversary of Sidney's mom's death. In *Jaws*, vacationers scramble out of the water to avoid the shark. In *Top Gun*, Charlotte tells Maverick, "Take me to bed or lose me forever."

Minute 60 in *The Sixth Sense*: A teenager shows Cole the back of his blown-out skull — The Shocker.

In *The Godfather*, Michael tells Kate to go back to New Hampshire — he doesn't know if he'll see her again. In *Forrest Gump*, Forrest shows the President his buttocks wound. In *Die Hard*, John finds C-4 explosives. In *Speed*, the Captain tells Jack that there's a gap in the road ahead.

Case studies:

In *Juno*, Juno finds out that Paulie asked Katrina to the prom.

In *The Matrix*, the sentinel approaches the Nebuchadnezzar.

In *Halloween*, Lynda tells her boyfriend that "Lindsey is gone for the night," which means they can have sex in the house.

In *Being John Malkovich*, Craig attacks Lotte with a gun.

In *Pulp Fiction*, Mia tells Vincent the joke she wasn't going to tell him before.

EXERCISE SIX

Okay, let's find Minute 55's SIDESWIPE moment in Jerry Zucker's *Ghost*. Start your stopwatch when Sam (Patrick Swayze) tells Molly (Demi Moore) in her apartment, "Look, if it'll make you feel any better, I'll check this out." What's the Sideswipe toward the later part of that minute? Now, what's the Sideswipe in Minute 55 of Paul Verhoeven's *Total Recall*? Start when Melina (Rachel Ticotin) tells the blonde prostitute in the club, "Honey, take care of Tony, will ya?".

ENTERING DEATH VALLEY

MINUTE 61: PLUS MINUS

A positive turns into a negative, or a negative turns into positive.

The Plus Minus is another way to keep your audience on an emotional rollercoaster ride. It's the good-news-bad-news scenario, or vice-versa.

POSITIVE TO NEGATIVE

In *Spider-Man,* Osborn tells the board their company's stock is up (+), but they tell him that they want to sell the company (-). In *Raiders of the Last Ark,* Indy is excited about getting the lid open (+), but then he notices the snakes (-). In *Jaws,* the shark (-) is really just a boy wearing a fake fin (+). In *The Sixth Sense,* the fiancé smiles when she sees Anna's ring on display (+), but frowns when her boyfriend asks for something "plainer" (-). In *Scream,* Sidney drives Tatum to the party (+), but Gale Weathers secretly follows them (-). In *Little Miss Sunshine,* Olive says Frank will get into heaven (+), but soon after a car almost hits them and the van's horn won't shut off (-). In *The Godfather,* Michael goes to see his father (+) but finds out there are no guards protecting him outside (-). In *Star Wars,* Luke does well with the light saber (+), but then the practice-blaster zaps him (-). In *Forrest Gump,* Forrest exits the bus in DC in his military uniform (+), but finds himself at an anti-war rally (-).

NEGATIVE TO POSITIVE

In *Die Hard,* the newscaster glares at the reporter (-), but then smiles at the camera and pretends nothing is wrong (+). It looks like they're going to die in *Speed* (-), but then Jack thinks there might be an incline they can jump (+).

During Minute 61 in *Tootsie*: Michael chats with his love interest Julie (+), but she throws a drink in his face (-) — Plus Minus.

What's the Plus Minus in our case studies?

In *Juno*, Juno leaves Leah after a relatively positive chat (+), but then she finds Paulie and yells at him (-).

In *The Matrix*, the sentinel closes in on the Nebuchadnezzar (-), but then flies away (+).

In *Halloween*, Lynda and her boyfriend have sex (+), but the phone interrupts them (-).

In *Being John Malkovich*, Craig forces (-) Lotte to set up a date with Maxine, and Maxine agrees (+).

In *Pulp Fiction*, Vincent goes from being scared (-) to smiling at Mia's joke (+).

MINUTE 62: FLIRTIN' WITH DISASTER

The band Molly Hatchet had a hit with their song "Flirtin With Disaster." I'd like to borrow the southern fried rock tune for this minute because it sums up 62 perfectly. Here are a number of examples of how movies flirt with disaster....

In *Jaws*, the local girl sees a shark fin in the pond. In *Top Gun*, Iceman cuts Maverick off. In *Little Miss Sunshine*, a cop stops the family. Chris's friend, in *Match Point*, says he saw Chris in an area of town that he shouldn't have been in. In *Knocked Up*, Debbie thinks Pete is cheating on her. Hans realizes John has the detonator in *Die Hard*. In *Tootsie*, the director gets upset when he finds out that "Dorothy" coached Julie. In *Speed*, the armed bus approaches the gap in the road.

Minute 62 in *Spider-Man*: Peter spies Harry and Mary Jane flirting with each other — Flirtin' With Disaster.

And how do our case studies flirt with disaster?

In *Juno*, Paulie scolds Juno.

In *The Matrix*, Neo drinks with Cypher (the man who will betray him).

In *Halloween*, Michael Myers walks into the room while the teenagers have sex.

In *Being John Malkovich*, Craig locks Lotte inside the monkey cage.

In *Pulp Fiction*, an ominous looking military man comes to visit young Butch.

MINUTE 63: ALLY ATTACK

Bad guy, or secondary bad guy, deeply affects hero's ally or love interest.

Not only does the bad guy attack the hero, now he takes a swipe at the hero's ally as well. *Will he stop at nothing?* I call this moment Ally Attack. The bad guy who executes this attack can be the out-and-out bad guy, like the shark in *Jaws*, or he can be an ally who's competing for the girl, like Harry in *Spider-Man*. Or he can be a temporary bad guy added during this minute to briefly affect the ally, or love interest, in some way. No matter the case, some kind of bad guy appears, and usually in these forms:

COMPETING FOR THE GIRL
Harry tries to kiss Mary Ann in *Spider-Man*. Belloq convinces Marion to put on a pretty white dress in *Raiders of the Lost Ark*. Gale Weathers flirts with Deputy Dewey in *Scream*.

OUT-AND-OUT BAD GUY
In *Top Gun*, Iceman's jet-wash G-forces affect Goose. In *Star Wars*, Tarkin orders his men to terminate Leia. In *Die Hard*, Hans's mission deeply affects Sgt. Al.

During Minute 63 in *Jaws*: Brody's son goes into shock after seeing the shark eat a man — Ally Attack.

COPS USED AS BAD GUYS

In *Little Miss Sunshine*, the cop tells Richard to put his hands on the car. In *The Godfather*, the police order the bodyguards to leave Michael's father all alone.

TEMPORARY BAD GUY

In *Speed*, the gap in the road deeply affects Annie and the passengers (they might die).

And how does the bad guy affect the hero's ally, or love interest, in our cast studies?

In *Juno*, Juno's pregnancy frustrates Paulie (TEMPORARY BAD GUY).

In *The Matrix*, Neo talks with Cypher, who secretly loves Trinity (COMPETING FOR THE GIRL).

In *Halloween*, Michael Myers scares Lynda's boyfriend with the creaking door (OUT-AND-OUT BAD GUY).

After hearing Craig's voice in his head, Malkovich freaks out while making love to Maxine in *Being John Malkovich* (COMPETING FOR THE GIRL).

In *Pulp Fiction*, the military man (the bad guy) tells young Butch a story that deeply affects him — a story about his dad's watch (TEMPORARY BAD GUY).

MINUTE 64: BAD GUY THREAT

Bad Guy, or secondary bad guy, threatens hero in some way.

The bad guy keeps up the pressure by posing a threat....

For example, in *Jaws*, Brody stares at the ocean where the shark roams. In *Top Gun*, Iceman's jet-wash causes Maverick to go into a flat spin. The Green Goblin throws bombs in *Spider-Man*. Indy is face-to-face with an about-to-strike snake in *Raiders of the Lost Ark*. Anna's new suitor threatens Malcolm's security in their relationship in *The Sixth Sense*. In *Scream*, Gale Weathers' attendance at the party threatens Sidney. In *Little Miss Sunshine*, the cop gives Richard a threatening look when he discovers the gay porn magazine.

In *The Godfather*, the nurse threatens Michael. In *Knocked Up*, Ben (the bad guy in this case) confesses that he thought of bolting for Canada when he found out Alison was pregnant, which threatens Alison's security. In *Star Wars*, a ship fires at the Millennium Falcon. In *Forrest Gump*, a Black Panther threatens Forrest. In *Die Hard*, the bad guys start drilling into the vault. In *Tootsie*, Michael finds out the director just fired another actor. In *Speed*, the speedometer slows down, threatening their lives.

And how does the bad guy threaten the hero in our case studies?

In *Juno*, the pregnancy (bad guy) threatens Juno's happiness.

In *The Matrix*, Cypher agrees to betray everyone for a life of ignorant bliss.

In *Halloween*, Michael Myers (bad guy) grabs Lynda's boyfriend (the hero in this case), then kills him.

In *Being John Malkovich*, Craig (the bad guy in this case) threatens Lotte to take over Malkovich's body.

In *Pulp Fiction*, the enemy, in the military man's story, threatens Butch's grandad's life.

MINUTE 65: THE RESISTANCE

Hero or ally attacks/resists the bad guy.

The bad guys have been putting on the pressure, in some form, during the last three minutes. Now it's time for the hero, or his ally, to fight back. This is called The Resistance.

The Resistance during Minute 65 in *Spider-Man*: Spider-Man attacks Green Goblin.

In *Raiders of the Lost Ark*, Indy squirts gas onto the snakes and torches them. In *Jaws*, Brody insists the mayor pay the ten grand to get Quint to kill the shark. In *Top Gun*, Maverick resists giving over Goose's body. In *The Sixth Sense*, Malcolm resists Cole's request for help. In *Scream*, Tatum resists the scary noises, made by the killer, in the basement.

In *The Godfather*, Michael resists the enemy by hiding his father. In *Forrest Gump*, Forrest tackles the guy who slapped Jenny.

In *Die Hard*, Sgt. Al resists his antagonistic superior. In *Tootsie*, Michael resists Jeff's urgings to not go with Julie to the farm.

And what is The Resistance in our case studies?

In *Juno*, Juno resists Mark and her attraction to him.

In *The Matrix*, Cypher scolds Mister Smith when he asks for the access codes.

In *Halloween*, Lynda scolds Michael Myers (who pretends to be Bob).

In *Being John Malkovich*, Charlie (ally) resists Malkovich's explanation that he wants to give up freaky Maxine.

In *Pulp Fiction*, Butch's dad, in the story, resists the enemy and hides the watch.

MINUTE 66: POSITIVE STEP

Hero does something positive toward his goal.

The hero keeps on the attack, making favorable strides forward on his mission. This is a Positive Step for him, and for the audience....

In *Spider-Man*, Spider-Man saves a boy. In *Raiders of the Lost Ark*, Indy closes in on the ark. In *Forrest Gump*, Forrest tells Jenny he wants to be her boyfriend. Olive plays a game to connect with her brother in *Little Miss Sunshine*. In *The Sixth Sense*, Malcolm studies his old session recordings. In *The Godfather*, Michael tells Enzo to go and stand outside (to help guard his father).

In *Match Point*, Chris pours massaging oil on Nola under candlelight. In *Die Hard*, Holly asks Hans to help the pregnant woman. In *Tootsie*, Michael drives with Julie to her father's farm. In *Speed*, Jack gets the bus to the airport so they can circle safely.

What Positive Step does the hero make in our case studies?

In *Juno*, Juno lays her head on Mark's chest.

In *The Matrix*, Neo eats to strengthen his body.

In *Halloween*, Laurie talks with Lynda over the phone.

In *Being John Malkovich*, Malkovich follows Maxine to work (to find out what's going on).

In *Pulp Fiction*, Butch steps toward the ring to fight.

MINUTE 67: HERO AFFECT

Hero does something that will immediately or eventually affect the main bad guy.

The hero is on a roll. Let's keep up his momentum during this minute by showing the hero affecting the main bad guy in some way....

In *Raiders of the Lost Ark*, Indy lifts the lid where the ark is kept. In *Spider-Man*, Spider-Man blinds Green Goblin and yanks out his flying machine wires. In *Scream*, Tatum throws a bottle at the killer and injures him. In *Jaws*, Brody tells Quint he's hired (which will soon affect the shark). In *The Sixth Sense*, Malcolm rewinds the tape after hearing strange noises. In *The Godfather*, Michael makes Enzo look like a bodyguard, which makes the enemy keep driving.

Holly avoids giving her married name to Hans in *Die Hard*. In *Tootsie*, "Dorothy" rides on the tractor with Julie's father (the bad guy who likes her in this case). In *Speed*, Jack pisses off the bomber over on the phone.

And what about our case studies?

In *The Matrix*, Neo goes to meet The Oracle (which will eventually affect Mr. Smith).

In *Halloween*, Laurie talks on the phone as Michael Myers silently listens in.

In *Being John Malkovich*, Malkovich follows Maxine into the building where the portal is.

In *Pulp Fiction*, Butch kills the guy he boxed, which causes Marsellus to loose lots of money.

Minute 67 in *Juno*: Juno scolds Mark for wanting to leave Vanessa — Hero Affect.

MINUTE 68: ALLY AID

Ally or love interest takes a positive/significant step towards hero.

I call this minute Ally Aid because, sure, the ally took a beating from the bad guy a few minutes back, but the ally is there for the hero, supposedly, through thick and thin. Let's see how....

LOVE INTEREST
In *Raiders of the Lost Ark,* Marion pulls a knife on Belloq (showing her loyalty to Indy). "I'll be there if you need me," Charlotte tells Maverick in *Top Gun*. Billy approaches Sidney to talk in *Scream*. In *Forrest Gump*, Jenny walks with Forrest. In *Tootsie*, Julie hangs out with "Dorothy" in the kitchen. Annie smiles at Jack and says, "Don't forget us" in *Speed*.

ALLY

In *The Sixth Sense*, Malcolm hears a distressed voice speaking in Latin (the cassette is Malcolm's ally in this case). Sheryl walks toward Dwayne to comfort him in *Little Miss Sunshine*. Han opens the smuggle-door to let Luke and Obi-Wan out in *Star Wars*. Sgt. Al tries to help John by holding back the police attack in *Die Hard*.

And how does this play out for our case studies?

In *Juno*, Mark expresses his feelings to Juno (a significant step toward Juno).

In *The Matrix*, Trinity listens as Neo expresses his feelings.

In *Halloween*, Dr. Loomis sees the mental hospital's car and runs toward it.

In *Being John Malkovich*, Malkovich runs after Craig and demands to know, "What's going on?"

In *Pulp Fiction*, Mia thanks Vincent for dinner.

MINUTE 69: CAPTIVATING CONCERN

Concern makes a re-appearance during Minute 69, but this time with more at stake. That's why I call it the Captivating Concern....

For example, in *Raiders of the Lost Ark*, Belloq and Marion show *concern* when the Nazi pulls out an ominous-looking object. In *Match Point*, Nola tells Chris she's pregnant. In *Spider-Man*, Harry shows *concern* over Mary Jane calling Spider-Man "incredible." In *Jaws*, Quint is *concerned* that Brody and Hooper want to go with him. In *The Sixth Sense*, Cole is *concerned* about Malcolm, "Are you wiggin' out?" he asks. In *Scream*, Randy shows *concern* when Billy takes Sidney upstairs.

In *Little Miss Sunshine*, Sheryl shows deep *concern* for her son who just lost his dream of flying. In *Knocked Up*, Alison shows *concern* because Ben wasn't there for her during the earthquake. In *Star Wars*, the soldier shows *concern* when the Stormtrooper's transmitter goes out.

Minute 69's Captivating Concern in *Top Gun*: Goose's wife cries because Goose is dead.

In *Forrest Gump*, Jenny is *concerned* that Forrest doesn't understand that they have very different lives. In *Die Hard*, Sgt. Al shows *concern* when the cops prepare to enter the building. In *Tootsie*, Julie's father shows *concern* when the swing breaks. In *Speed*, the Captain shows *concern* when Jack tells him the bomber will blow up the bus if the passengers are taken off.

And how is *concern* shown in our case studies?

In *Juno*, Vanessa shows concern when Juno skirts by her upset.

In *The Matrix*, Trinity shows concern when Neo asks her what The Oracle told her.

In *Halloween*, Dr. Loomis shows concern when he sees the mental hospital logo.

In *Being John Malkovich*, Malkovich shows concern when he enters the portal.

In *Pulp Fiction*, Butch shows concern when he hears he killed the other boxer.

MINUTE 70: NEW JOURNEY

When the characters embark on a New Journey, many questions are raised that need to be answered: Will they survive it? Will they be hurt? Will they ultimately succeed? Wanting to know the answer to these questions keeps us watching, or reading....

In *Spider-Man*, Green Goblin reveals himself to Osborn (they will go on a new journey of evil together). In *Raiders of the Lost Ark*, Indy asks the men to raise the ark out of the tomb (a new journey begins with the ark). In *Jaws*, Quint, Brody and Hooper load equipment for their new journey to kill the shark. In *Top Gun*, Maverick watches Goose's wife leave, beginning a new journey without his best friends. Now that Malcolm believes Cole, in *The Sixth Sense*, Malcolm wants to know what the ghosts want when they talk to him (a new journey of finding out what their purpose is).

In *Scream*, Sidney and Billy try to mend their relationship (a new journey in their relationship). In *The Godfather*, Sonny orders a hit on the Tattaglia family (a new journey of revenge). In *Match Point*, Chris and Nola wonder what to do about her pregnancy (a new journey for them). In *Star Wars*, Obi-Wan heads deeper into the Death Star to shut down the tractor beam (a new journey for him).

In *Forrest Gump*, Forrest embarks on his new journey as a ping-pong player. In *Die Hard*, the cops run toward the building to enter it (a new journey for them). In *Tootsie*, Julie tells "Dorothy" a new story about her father (a new journey of honesty and intimacy between them). In *Speed*, Jack decides to ride the low-rider underneath the bus (a dangerous new journey).

What new journey is embarked on in our case studies?

In *Juno*, Mark wonders aloud to Vanessa if this is the right thing (Vanessa has to prepare for a possible new journey without a baby).

In *The Matrix*, Neo opens The Oracle's apartment door (his new journey toward the truth).

In *Halloween*, Laurie walks toward Lynda's house to see if she's okay (a new journey for her).

In *Pulp Fiction*, Butch asks the sexy cab driver for a cigarette and they chat (she takes him on a new journey of life on the run).

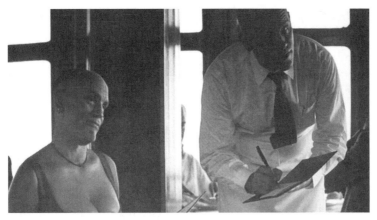

Minute 70 in *Being John Malkovich*: Malkovich finds himself in a world of Malkoviches — the New Journey for him.

EXERCISE SEVEN

Minute 66 — THE POSITIVE STEP. What positive step does David (Bruce Willis) take toward his wife in M. Night Shyamalan's *Unbreakable*? The minute starts just after the movie cuts to David and his wife having dinner at the fancy restaurant. In Chris & Paul Weitz's *About a Boy*, how does Will (Hugh Grant) take a positive step toward Marcus in the early part of Minute 66? Start your stopwatch just as Will and Rachel take Marcus into Rachel's son's bedroom.

MINUTE 71: BAD TO THE BONE

Bad guy, or secondary bad guy, shows aggression.

Not to be ignored, the bad guy goes on the attack again, in one way or another, for the next seven minutes. He just can't help himself because he's just like that George Thorogood song "Bad To The Bone." And he gets badder by the minute....

In *Spider-Man*, Green Goblin speaks angrily to Osborn. In *Raiders of the Lost Ark*, Belloq yells down to Indy. In *Jaws*, Quint sings offensive songs and is verbally abusive. Malcolm sees Anna's new boyfriend (the bad guy in this case) exiting her house in *The Sixth Sense*. In *Scream*, Billy makes sexual advances toward Sidney (sexual aggression).

In *The Godfather*, Tom yells at Sonny for taking it personally. Nola yells at Chris in *Match Point*. In *Knocked Up*, the baby (the bad guy in this case) has grown bigger in size. In *Star Wars*, Tarkin schedules Leia for execution. In *Forrest Gump*, the Asian ping-pong player (the bad guy) hits the ball hard at Forrest. The bad guys ready their guns in *Die Hard*. Julie's father says he'll stay up with "Dorothy" in *Tootsie*. In *Speed*, the bomb counts down.

How does the bad guy show aggression toward our case studies?

In *Juno*, Vanessa tells Mark (the bad guy) to grow up.

In *The Matrix*, the boy politely scolds Neo, telling him not to bend the spoon.

In *Halloween*, no one answers the door (because they were murdered by Michael Myers).

In *Being John Malkovich*, Malkovich pushes another version of himself out of the way.

In *Pulp Fiction*, Butch (the bad guy in this case) says he doesn't feel the least bit bad about killing the boxer.

MINUTE 72: BADDER TO THE BONE

Bad guy, or secondary bad guy, shows more aggression.

In *Spider-Man*, Green Goblin crashes into Jameson's office. In *Jaws*, Quint escalates his verbal tirade. In *Top Gun*, Maverick's fellow pilots (the bad guys in this case) order him to engage. Ghosts turn the air cold around Cole in *The Sixth Sense*. In *Scream*, Billy lays Sidney onto the bed (more sexual aggression).

Minute 72 in *Raiders of the Lost Ark*: Major Toht throws Marion into the snake-filled tomb with Indy — Badder To The Bone.

In *The Godfather*, Tom yells at Sonny even more for wanting to kill the police captain. In *Match Point*, Chloe asks Chris if he's having an affair. In *Knocked Up*, Debbie goes to spy on Pete, who may be cheating on her (either of them could be the bad guy in this case — Debbie for spying, and Pete for lying). In *Star Wars*, Chewbacca growls when Luke tries to put handcuffs on him. In *Forrest Gump*, Lt. Dan yells at Forrest. In *Die Hard*, bad guys shoot out the cops' lights. In *Tootsie*, Julie's father flirts with "Dorothy" (unwanted sexual aggression). In *Speed*, the bus's tires hit debris and shake the bomb.

And how do the bad guys show even more aggression in our case studies?

In *Juno*, Juno cries because of what bad guy Mark did.

In *The Matrix*, the boy waits to see if Neo can bend the spoon (mild aggression toward Neo's ignorance).

In *Halloween*, Michael Myers makes a noise that scares Laurie.

In *Being John Malkovich*, Malkovich threatens to sue Craig.

In *Pulp Fiction*, Butch speaks aggressively to Scotty.

MINUTE 73:
BADDEST TO THE BONE

Bad guy, or secondary bad guy, ratchets up aggression even more.

In *Spider-Man*, Green Goblin knocks out Spidey. In *Jaws*, Quint makes even more fun of Hooper, and Hooper yells at Brody for knocking over the compressed air. In *Top Gun*, Maverick's new co-pilot yells at Maverick for not engaging. In *Raiders of the Lost Ark*, the Nazis seal Indy and Marion inside the tomb.

In *The Godfather*, the police captain wants a meeting with Michael. Chris lies and says he's not having an affair in *Match Point*. In *Knocked Up*, Debbie enters the house where Pete's car is parked (again, either of them could be the bad guy in this case).

In *Star Wars*, the Death Star workers walk dangerously close to Luke, Han, and Chewbacca. In *Die Hard*, the bad guys shoot two cops. Julie's father flirts with "Dorothy" even more (more unwanted sexual aggression). In *Speed*, debris (the bad guy) knocks Jack off course and threatens his life.

Case studies:

In *Juno*, Juno lays on the hood of her car, completely alone (loneliness is the bad guy).

In *The Matrix*, The Oracle tells Neo not to worry about the vase, which he soon breaks (polite aggression toward Neo's ignorance).

In *Halloween*, Michael Myers lurks around the next corner.

In *Being John Malkovich*, Lotte wants to be let out of the cage.

In *Pulp Fiction*, Bad guy Butch flirts with the sexy cab driver.

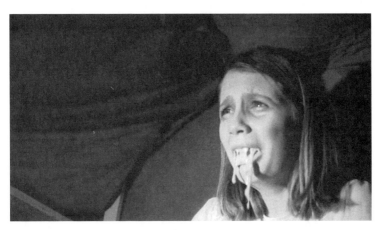

Minute 73 in *The Sixth Sense*: A vomiting ghost enters Cole's safe space — Baddest To The Bone.

MINUTE 74: PUT INTO PERIL

Hero and/or ally is put into peril.

By this time in the movie, the hero and ally are like avatars or surrogates for the audience member — an extension of themselves. When they are Put Into Peril, so is the viewer. And you put them into peril by making things fall apart.

LIFE IN PERIL

In *Spider-Man*, Green Goblin paralyzes Spider-Man. In *Raiders of the Lost Ark,* snakes close in on Indy and Marion as their torch dwindles. In *Scream*, someone bangs on Gale Weathers' van door. In *The Godfather*, Michael is put into peril by agreeing to kill the police captain.

In *Star Wars*, the soldiers point guns at Luke, Han, and Chewbacca. In *Forrest Gump*, Lt. Dan drinks too much and is angry at Jesus (his life and salvation are in peril). In *Die Hard*, John hears the bad guys coming (his life is in peril). In *Speed*, the cable breaks and puts Jack's life into peril. In *The Sixth Sense*, the dead girl speaks to Cole (his life is in peril).

RESPECT IN PERIL

In *Jaws*, Hooper is in peril of losing Quint's respect.

CAREER IN PERIL

In *Top Gun*, Maverick quits, which puts his career into peril.

DREAM IN PERIL

In *Little Miss Sunshine*, the contest coordinator says they are too late (putting Olive's dream in peril).

RELATIONSHIP IN PERIL

In *Match Point*, Chris bares his soul to his tennis friend (his marriage is in peril because of his affair). In *Knocked Up*, Debbie catches Pete playing fantasy baseball (their marriage is in peril).

SECRET IN PERIL

In *Tootsie*, Michael (as "Dorothy") has to sleep next to Julie in his makeup.

What's put into peril for our case studies?

In *Juno*, Mark called the divorce lawyer, putting Vanessa's RELATIONSHIP IN PERIL, and Vanessa's DREAM IN PERIL.

In *The Matrix*, Neo doubts he's "The One," which puts him and mankind into peril (LIFE IN PERIL).

In *Halloween*, Laurie sees Annie's dead body in front of the headstone (LIFE IN PERIL).

In *Being John Malkovich*, Lotte can't get out of the cage (RELATIONSHIP IN PERIL).

In *Pulp Fiction*, Butch hides out in the hotel room while Marsellus has his men look for him (LIFE IN PERIL).

MINUTE 75:
SKULL & CROSSBONES

Death comes on strong in these next two minutes, making his boney appearance in eight different ways, which we'll explore below. The next two minutes are a heavy reminder that just like in real life, the things most precious to us — life and love and hopes and dreams — can be snatched away at any moment, thus the title "Skull & Crossbones."

SYMBOLS OF DEATH
In *The Sixth Sense*, Cole sees a graveyard and gasps. In *The Godfather*, Michael holds the gun that he will kill the police captain with.

Minute 75 in *Raiders of the Lost Ark*: Marion finds skeletons — Skull & Crossbones.

THREAT OF DEATH

In *Jaws*, Quint notices his fishing line creaking (the shark/death approaches). In *Star Wars*, soldiers try to kill Luke and Han. In *Speed*, Jack is near death.

DEATH OF A RELATIONSHIP

In *Top Gun*, Charlotte is upset that Maverick didn't say goodbye; she's moving to Washington. In *Match Point*, Chris tells Nola he's leaving with Chloe's family for three weeks — death of their relationship makes its first appearance. In *Knocked Up*, Debbie and Pete's relationship spirals downward.

DEATH OF A GOOD REPUTATION

In *Spider-Man*, newspapers say Green Goblin and Spider-Man terrorize the city (death of Spidey's good reputation).

DEATH OF A DREAM

In *Little Miss Sunshine*, Olive's dream seems to be crushed.

DEATH OF LIFE

In *Die Hard*, the bad guys destroy the cop's tank and kill the driver. In *Rashomon*, the bandit kills the husband.

TALK OF DEATH

In *Tootsie*, Julie talks about her dead mother.

DEATH OF BELIEF

In *Forrest Gump*, Lt. Dan's belief in God is dead.

What's the Skull & Crossbone's moment in our case studies?

In *Juno*, Juno tells her dad she's losing her faith in humanity (DEATH OF BELIEF).

In *The Matrix*, Neo says he's not The One (DEATH OF BELIEF).

In *Halloween*, Laurie finds Lynda and her boyfriend's dead bodies (DEATH OF LIFE).

In *Being John Malkovich*, hunters try to capture Lotte's monkey (DEATH OF LIFE).

Though Butch acts like nothing is wrong in *Pulp Fiction*, he knows Marsellus wants to kill him (DEATH OF LIFE).

MINUTE 76: THE GRIM REAPER

And as the hero walks deeper into the Valley Of Death (to paraphrase The Lord's Prayer), the black-hooded Grim Reaper, in some way, taps him on the shoulder with the tip of his scythe. Here's a few ways he does that during Minute 76:

SYMBOLS OF DEATH
In *Raiders of the Lost Ark*, the skulls make Marion scream. Friends and family, dressed in black, attend a wake in *The Sixth Sense*. Richard asks if there's a funeral home nearby in *Little Miss Sunshine*.

THREAT OF DEATH
The shark (death) takes Quint's bait in *Jaws*. In *The Godfather*, Michael fires the gun to practice killing the police captain. The wounded cops scream in pain in *Die Hard*. They find out the bus is leaking gas in *Speed*. In *Star Wars*, the enemy closes in.

TALK OF DEATH
Julie talks more about her dead mother in *Tootsie*. Randy says, "Listen up, they found Principal Himbry dead" in *Scream*.

DEATH OF A RELATIONSHIP
In *Spider-Man*, Peter asks out Mary Jane, but she's going out with Harry. Maverick and Charlotte can't seem to mend their relationship in *Top Gun*. In *Match Point*, the trip is called off, but Chris doesn't tell Nola. Debbie says she doesn't want Pete at the house anymore in *Knocked Up*.

DEATH OF A DREAM
In *Forrest Gump*, Lt. Dan makes fun of Forrest's dream of running a shrimp boat (death of Forrest's dream).

Here are the stronger death appearances in our case studies:

In *Juno*, Juno doesn't know if two people can stay in love (DEATH OF BELIEF).

In *The Matrix*, The Oracle tells Neo that Morpheus will sacrifice his life (THREAT OF DEATH).

In *Halloween*, Michael Myers breaks through the door to try and kill Laurie (THREAT OF DEATH).

In *Being John Malkovich*, Maxine and Lotte's relationship starts to die (DEATH OF A RELATIONSHIP).

In *Pulp Fiction*, Butch's girlfriend says, "If they find us, they'll kill us, won't they?" (THREAT OF DEATH).

MINUTE 77: THE RUMBLE

The tension of death needs a release, and this is the minute where that happens. The release comes in the form of a fight. It's time to rumble, either physically or emotionally. Whichever one you choose, a fight breaks out either way....

The Rumble during Minute 77 of *Spider-Man*: Spidey fights the bad guys who are harassing Mary Jane.

PHYSICAL RUMBLE/FIGHT

In *Raiders of the Lost Ark*, Indy *fights* the German near the plane. In *Jaws*, Quint *fights* the shark. We see Jenny's black and blue eye in *Forrest Gump* (she had a *fight* with her boyfriend). John detonates the bomb in *Die Hard*.

EMOTIONAL RUMBLE/FIGHT

In *Top Gun*, Maverick resists (*fights*) Charlotte's offer of help. In *The Sixth Sense*, friends and family *fight* their grief. In *Little Miss Sunshine*, Frank sees that his writing nemesis has a best-seller, and he *fights* his urge to scream. In *The Godfather*, Tom and Sonny argue. Ben and Alison argue in *Knocked Up*. In *Star Wars,* Tarkin and Darth argue. In *Tootsie*, the producer calls "Dorothy" a pain in the ass (picks a *fight*).

What's The Rumble, or fight, in our case studies?

In *Juno*, Juno *wrestles* with her feelings about love.

In *The Matrix*, Neo *fights* his urge to tell Morpheus what The Oracle told him (EMOTIONAL FIGHT).

In *Halloween*, Laurie *screams* at her neighbors, but they won't help her (EMOTIONAL FIGHT).

In *Being John Malkovich*, Malkovich *yells* at Maxine (EMOTIONAL FIGHT).

In *Pulp Fiction*, Butch's girlfriend *yells* at him in the bathroom (EMOTIONAL FIGHT).

MINUTE 78: MYSTERY MISSION

Hero and ally interact; there's a mystery that needs to be solved.

Okay, death has made an appearance and it caused a fight, but now the screenwriter must plant something during the next couple of minutes to keep the viewer watching. What they do is create a Mystery Mission. Mystery creates curiosity and spurs *more* questions. That curiosity *has* to be satisfied. Those questions *have* to be answered.

For example, in *Spider-Man*, Mary Jane can't see Spidey's real face (her mission is to find out who he is). In *Jaws*, Hooper tells Quint he doesn't think it's the shark pulling the line — if it's not, what is it? In *Top Gun*, Maverick spots a picture of Metcalf with his father — did they know each other? In *Scream*, Dewey and Gale wonder why the cars are driving away so fast (their mission is to find out why).

In *Little Miss Sunshine*, the event volunteer questions Olive about her song selection — what is the song he's so curious about? In *The Godfather*, they don't know where the meeting will be held. In *Match Point*, Chris hides the fact that he really didn't leave on holiday — will Nola find out? In *Knocked Up*, Ben and Alison's argument escalates — will their relationship make it?

In *Star Wars*, Luke asks C-3PO if there's some way out — is there? In *Tootsie*, Michael and his agent talk on the phone — what are they going to do about his situation? In *Speed*, Harold and the officers enter the bomber's house — where is he?

The Mystery Mission during Minute 78 in *The Sixth Sense*: The dead girl gives Cole a box — what's in it?

What is the Mystery Mission in our case studies?

In *Juno*, Juno's dad wonders if Juno was talking about him. Was she?

In *The Matrix*, Tank looks at the computer screen and says, "What is that?"

In *Halloween*, Laurie orders the boy to go upstairs. Is Michael Myers inside the house?

In *Being John Malkovich*, Craig hides inside Malkovich's mind. Will he be found out by Maxine?

In *Pulp Fiction*, will Marsellus find Butch?

MINUTE 79: MYSTERY MISSION 2

Hero and/or ally(s) continue to engage/interact; more mystery.

In *Star Wars*, Luke and Han wonder how they are going to get out of their situation. John and Sgt. Al chat on the walkie-talkie in *Die Hard* — where is John hiding? Michael and Jeff talk in *Tootsie* — what's Michael going to do about his situation? As Jack and Annie continue to ride on the bus in *Speed*, they wonder: Will it blow up?

In *Raiders of the Lost Ark*, Indy and Marion continue to fight Germans — will they survive? In *Jaws*, Quint and Hooper fight — is the shark nearby? What's the mysterious classified information in *Top Gun*? Cole interacts with the dead girl's father in *The Sixth Sense* — what's in the box? Dewey and Gale find Neil Prescott's car in *Scream* — "What's he doing here?"

The family talks about how they will kill the police captain in *The Godfather* — how will they do it? Chris lies to Nola in *Match Point* — will his wife find out about his affair? Alison kicks Ben out of the car in *Knocked Up* — will their relationship survive?

Mystery Mission 2 in *The Matrix*: During Minute 79, everyone stops when Neo says he experienced *déjà vu* — what does that mean?

What's the Mystery Mission in our case studies?

In *Juno*, Juno leaves Paulie a message to check the mail — what's in the mailbox?

In *Halloween*, Laurie holds the knife (her ally in this case) — is Michael Myers dead?

In *Being John Malkovich*, Lotte shows up at Dr. Lester's house — he wonders why she's there.

In *Pulp Fiction*, Butch and his girlfriend chat in the bathroom — will Marsellus find them?

MINUTE 80: TICK TICK BOOM

I call this minute Tick Tick Boom. Why? Because just like a stick of dynamite with a timer attached, the tension has built since Minute 70's New Journey began, which has taken the hero through the Valley Of Death, a fight, and a couple unanswered questions. The frustration and stress is too much and the dynamite has finally ignited. As a result, an EXPLOSION surprises the hero or ally. Sometimes it's an actual explosion. Most of the time, though, it's an emotional explosion. Take note of how much yelling and screaming occurs during this minute.

EMOTIONAL EXPLOSION

In *Jaws*, Quint yells at Hooper. In *Match Point*, Nola screams at Chris on the street. In *Knocked Up*, Alison and Ben scream at each other at the doctor's office. In *Star Wars*, Luke yells at Han for trying to blast his way through the garbage walls. In *Forrest Gump*, Lt. Dan screams at the girls and kicks them out of his room. In *Die Hard*, John yells over the walkie-talkie. In *Speed*, Jack screams in frustration.

Other types of emotional explosions:
The audience bursts into heartfelt applause in *Little Miss Sunshine*. Sonny and Michael kiss and hug in *The Godfather*. In *Top Gun*, Metcalf tells Maverick that his father saved three planes before he died (an emotional bomb for Maverick). Julie freaks out about her decision to break up with Ron in *Tootsie*.

ACTUAL EXPLOSION

In *Spider-Man*, the apartment Spidey enters *explodes*! In *Raiders of the Lost Ark*, the leaking gas *explodes*!

And how about our case studies?

In *Juno*, Juno tells Paulie that she loves him and that her heart pounds every time she sees him (EMOTIONAL EXPLOSION).

Bullets rip apart Mouse's body in *The Matrix* (ACTUAL EXPLOSION).

In *Halloween*, Dr. Loomis yells at the sheriff, "Michael Myers is here!" (EMOTIONAL EXPLOSION)

In *Being John Malkovich*, Lotte raises her voice and says she wants to be John Malkovich (EMOTIONAL EXPLOSION).

In *Pulp Fiction*, Butch screams because of a bad dream; there are also explosions on TV (EMOTIONAL AND ACTUAL EXPLOSIONS).

NOTE: Depending on how long your story is, somewhere between Minutes 80 and 110 is what I call the FINAL QUEST.
It's the last push toward the final battle place. During Minute
80 in *Halloween*, Dr. Loomis yells out to the sheriff, "Michael
Myers is here!" Knowing where he is, they begin their Final
Quest to capture him. During Minute 105 in *Star Wars*, the reb-
els head out for their secret attack (Final Quest) to destroy the
Death Star. During Minute 89 in *Little Miss Sunshine*, the stage
manager tells Olive that it's time for her to perform, her Final
Quest to win the contest. During Minute 110 in *Knocked Up*,
Ben and Allison rush to the hospital so she can give birth (their
Final Quest in the pregnancy). During Minute 97 in *Raiders of
the Lost Ark*, Indy heads toward the island on the submarine on
his Final Quest to capture the ark.

EXERCISE EIGHT

THE RUMBLE happens during Minute 77. What is the fight
about when Hannah has lunch with her two sisters in Woody
Allen's *Hannah and Her Sisters*? Start the stopwatch when the sisters are having lunch and Holly (Dianne Wiest) says "Let's face
it here, I gotta latch onto something." What do Jack and Wendy
(Jack Nicholson and Shelley Duvall) argue/Rumble about at
the beginning of Minute 66 in Stanley Kubrick's *The Shining*?
(The minute starts when the little boy opens his mouth wide
and envisions the lobby of blood).

⏰ THE PENULTIMATUM
MINUTE 81: SURPRISED HERO

Bad guy or ally surprises hero.

Not only does the explosion surprise the hero or ally, the surprises keep coming over the next two minutes. If your hero is surprised, your audience will be too.

Minute 81 in *Jaws*: The shark pops out of the water — Surprised Hero.

In *Star Wars*, the creature yanks Luke underneath the water (SURPRISE!). In *Scream*, the killer *surprises* Sidney and kills Billy. In *Top Gun*, Maverick sees Charlotte's "For Rent" sign (she already left, much to his *surprise*). In *The Sixth Sense*, the mother (in the VHS tape) *surprises* the girl. In *Little Miss Sunshine*, what's happening on stage *surprises* Richard. In *Match Point*, Nola's request *surprises* Chris. In *Forrest Gump*, Nixon resigns as President (SURPRISE!). In *Tootsie*, Ron *surprises* Michael by calling him "Honey." In *Spider-Man*, Spidey tries to save the old lady, but it's really the Green Goblin!

What surprises our hero in our case studies?

In *Juno*, Paulie kisses Juno (SURPRISE!).

Much to his *surprise*, S.W.A.T. agents find the wall Neo hides behind in *The Matrix*.

In *Halloween*, the kids scream when they see Michael Myers (SURPRISE!).

In *Being John Malkovich*, Dr. Lester *surprises* Lotte by telling her he found the vessel.

In *Pulp Fiction*, Butch's girlfriend jumps on him in bed (SURPRISE!).

MINUTE 82: SURPRISE-SURPRISE

I once visited "Dracula's Castle" in Wildwood, New Jersey — a boardwalk horror funhouse teenage friends and I were curious about. As we felt our way through the dark hallways, passing tableaus of dungeon scenes and guillotines, an occasional funhouse employee, costumed as a demon or ghoul, would dart out at us. Toward the end of the twelve-minute tour, however, they hit us with two surprises in a row: A hissing vampire jumped out of a concealed compartment, and a werewolf barked out a blood-curdling howl above us. The vampire startled me, yes, but the werewolf *really* surprised me — so much so that I yelped. That's what Minute 82's Surprise-Surprise is about: To follow up with another unexpected scare.

In *Match Point*, Nola *surprises* Chris by saying that *she'll* tell Chloe about her pregnancy. In *Spider-Man*, Green Goblin throws a deadly disc at Spidey. In *Raiders of the Lost Ark*, Sallah *surprises* Indy by telling him the ark was loaded into a truck. In *Top Gun*, Maverick *surprises* the other pilots by not showing up for graduation. In *The Sixth Sense*, the mother pours poison into her daughter's soup and feeds it to her (SURPRISE!).

Scream's killer breaks through the attic door and grabs Sidney (SURPRISE!). Richard is *surprised* by how creepy the pageant is in *Little Miss Sunshine*. In *The Godfather*, the driver *surprises* Michael by passing a Jersey sign. In *Star Wars*, the walls start to close in (SURPRISE!). In *Forrest Gump*, Forrest gets his discharge papers (SURPRISE!). In *Die Hard*, Hans *surprises* John by calling him by name. In *Tootsie*, "Dorothy" says "Bullshit!", which *surprises* Ron. Jack is *surprised* to learn there's a camera on the bus.

What's the Surprise-Surprise for our case studies?

In *Juno*, Juno goes into labor (SURPRISE!).

In *The Matrix*, the agent breaks through the wall and grabs Neo (SURPRISE!).

In *Halloween*, Michael Myers breaks through the closet door (SURPRISE!).

In *Being John Malkovich*, Dr. Lester says he's going to permanently enter Malkovich's body when he turns 44 (SURPRISE!).

In *Pulp Fiction*, Butch can't find his watch (SURPRISE!).

MINUTE 83: GOTTA GO!

Hero hurries somewhere.

If we were strolling through the city and we saw someone sprinting down the sidewalk, we would stop for a few moments and watch, wouldn't we? What are they running away from? What are they hurrying toward? The screenwriter uses this same Gotta Go! technique to hold the audience's attention.

In *Scream*, Sidney *hurries* toward the van. In *Spider-Man*, Spidey *hurries* to make the party. In *Jaws*, Brody, Quint and Hooper hurry to their posts. In *Top Gun*, Metcalf informs the pilots they must leave in a *hurry*. In *The Godfather*, the car does a one-eighty and *hurries* toward the restaurant.

In *Match Point*, Chris *hurries* to the gun cabinet. In *Star Wars*, C-3PO and R2-D2 *hurry* away from the Stormtrooper. In *Forrest Gump*, Forrest *hurries* home to Mama Gump. In *Tootsie*, Michael *hurries* from one room to the next with the crying baby. Jack tells the Captain to *hurry* and roll the tape in *Speed*. In *Rashomon*, the commoner *hurries* to retrieve the baby from the priest.

Minute 83 in *Raiders of the Lost Ark*: Indy hops onto a horse and *hurries* toward the Nazi truck — Gotta Go!

Where is the hero hurrying to in our case studies?

In *Juno*, Dad and Brenda *hurry* Juno to the hospital.

In *The Matrix*, Neo *hurries* down the shaft.

In *Halloween*, Laurie *hurries* toward the boy's room.

In *Being John Malkovich*, Dr. Lester *hurries* Lotte into the other room.

In *Pulp Fiction*, Butch hurriedly grabs the lamp to throw it (soon he will *hurry* to retrieve his watch).

MINUTE 84: GAP SUBTRACT

Gap between hero and bad guy/ally decreases.

If another person steps into our personal space, we have no choice but to pay attention. I call this the Gap Subtract. It forces a reaction in the hero. It works the same way for the audience during Minute 84....

Minute 84 in *Spider-Man*: Osborn enters Peter's room while Peter hides — Gap Subtract.

In *Top Gun*, MiGs close in on Maverick. In *Raiders of the Lost Ark*, Indy closes in on the Nazi trucks. In *Jaws*, the shark swims closer to the boat. In *Scream*, the killer closes in on Sidney. In *The Godfather*, Michael sits directly across from the bad guy and the police captain. In *Match Point*, Chloe closes in on Chris as he puts the gun into his bag. In *Star Wars*, the walls close in on Luke, Han, Leia and Chewbacca. In *Forrest Gump*, Forrest gets close to Bubba's grave to talk to him. In *Speed*, the gap between the bus and rescue bus decreases.

What is the Gap Subtract in our case studies?

In *Juno*, Paulie runs to the hospital to be with Juno.

In *The Matrix*, cops charge Morpheus.

In *Halloween*, Michael Myers closes the gap between himself and Laurie.

In *Being John Malkovich*, Craig (as Malkovich) gets closer to Maxine.

In *Pulp Fiction*, Butch steps closer to his girlfriend and apologizes.

MINUTE 85: BAD GUY BOO-BOO

I call this minute Bad Guy Boo-Boo, referring to what my friend's mom used to call scrapes on the knee or accidental burns. This is the minute we see hints that the bad guy is vulnerable. There's a chink in his armor. He has an Achilles' heel. When the audience sees this weakness, they'll think it just might be possible for the hero to defeat him. The audience will stick around to see if it actually happens.

In *Spider-Man*, Aunt May slaps Osborn's hand. The mean actor-kid in *The Sixth Sense* is hurt because he didn't get the lead role (Cole did). In *Raiders of the Lost Ark*, Indy slams into the Nazi's truck. In *Jaws*, Quint harpoons the shark. In *Scream*, the killer's chances are hurt when Sidney runs. In *Little Miss Sunshine*, the contestant's yodeling is terrible (Olive may have a chance to win after all).

In *The Godfather*, Michael's words hurt the bad guy betrayer. In *Match Point*, unruly Nola is hurt that Chris didn't tell Chloe yet. In *Knocked Up*, Pete is hurt that he can't do fun stuff with Debbie. In *Star Wars*, Obi-Wan hurts Darth's chances by advancing on the tractor beam controls. Julie breaks up with bad guy Ron in *Tootsie*.

What is the Bad Guy Boo-Boo in the case studies?

In *Juno*, Paulie decides not to look at his baby.

In *The Matrix*, Morpheus punches the S.W.A.T. agents.

In *Halloween*, Dr. Loomis shoots Michael Myers.

In *Being John Malkovich*, Malkovich gags.

In *Pulp Fiction*, Butch's girlfriend is upset because she forgot the watch.

MINUTE 86: WORRY WOUND

Something happens during Minute 86 that worries one of our main characters and wounds him, thus the title Worry Wound. And when a Worry Wound occurs, it has to be remedied in some way. As a result, the audience will stay in their seats to see how....

In *Match Point*, Chloe starts to unzip Chris's tennis bag, which causes him great worry (the shotgun is inside) and will *wound* his cover-up if she finds it. In *Little Miss Sunshine*, the other contestants' superior talents cause Richard great *worry* for his daughter, who might be *wounded* by defeat. They won't let the aging Alison and Debbie into the club in *Knocked Up*, which *worries* them and *wounds* their egos. In *Spider-Man*, Osborn's suspicion grows toward Peter (which worries Peter because Osborn could *wound* his efforts to keep his identity secret).

In *Raiders of the Lost Ark*, the German soldier climbs toward Indy (which *worries* him because the bigger man might *wound* him). In *Jaws*, the sun goes down, which *worries* Brody (because the shark might eat him in the darkness). In *Scream*, the blood *worries* Gale Weathers because the nearby killer might *wound* her too. In *Star Wars,* the approaching Stormtroopers *worry* Obi-Wan because they might *wound* his efforts. In *Speed*, the blown tire *worries* Jack because they might die.

Minute 86 in *Tootsie*: Worried Michael freaks out when Julie rejects his kiss, which wounds his romantic chances with her — Worry Wound.

What's the Worry Wound in our case studies?

In *Juno*, wounded Vanessa *worries* how she looks with the baby.

In *The Matrix*, Cypher shoots Tank and Dozer, which *worries* Neo — Cypher might kill him as well.

In *Halloween*, a *worried* Dr. Loomis sees that Michael Myers is gone — he will probably kill others. [*Halloween* ends here, but the *Something Startling Happens* beats continue for our longer movies.]

In *Being John Malkovich*, Craig *worries* that their moneymaking enterprise might be damaged.

In *Pulp Fiction*, Butch *worries* about returning to his apartment to retrieve his watch — the hitmen might kill him.

MINUTE 87: DAMAGE DONE

Bad guy provokes physical or emotional damage.

The bad guy may have been hurt a couple minutes ago, but this only made him angrier. He's going to retaliate here until there's Damage Done, especially during the next two minutes....

The dead body on her windshield causes Gale emotional damage in *Scream*. Osborn yells at his son in *Spider-Man*, and Mary Jane scolds Harry for not standing up for her (emotional damage). In *Jaws*, Quint and Hooper show each other their scars (physical and emotional damage).

In *Match Point*, Chloe says that she wants to meet Chris before the ballet, which puts more stress on his killing plans. In *Knocked Up*, the bouncer damages Debbie's ego by not letting her into the club. In *Forrest Gump*, drugs cause physical and emotional damage to Jenny. Hans's request creates anxiety for the Chief in *Die Hard*. In *Tootsie*, Julie rejects Michael, which causes him emotional damage. In *Speed*, the ramp leading to the road freaks out Annie.

Minute 87 in *Raiders of the Lost Ark*: The German soldier shoots Indy's arm — Damage Done.

How do the bad guys provoke damage in the case studies?

In *Juno*, Juno cries over the whole situation (emotional damage). [Juno ends here, but it's a happy ending because she reunites with Paulie.]

In *The Matrix*, Cypher betrays the group, saying he's tired of it all (damages their safety).

In *Being John Malkovich*, the agent yells at the secretary (emotional damage).

In *Pulp Fiction*, Butch is deeply concerned that one of Marsellus's hit men might be waiting for him (emotional and possible physical damage).

MINUTE 88:
DOUBLE DAMAGE DONE

Bad guy causes additional physical or emotional damage.

In *Spider-Man*, Green Goblin scares Aunt May. In *Raiders of the Lost Ark*, the German soldier punches Indy's wounded arm and throws him through the windshield. In *Jaws*, Hooper and Quint show each other more scars. The killer stabs Dewey, then chases Sidney in *Scream*. In *Knocked Up*, the bouncer tells Alison she's a bad parent and calls Debbie an "old ass."

In *Star Wars*, an overwhelming number of Stormtroopers fire at Han. In *Forrest Gump*, Jenny cradles herself after nearly committing suicide. Julie's father asks "Dorothy" out in *Tootsie*. The bomb blows up the bus and the plane in *Speed*. In *The Godfather*, the bad guy's words cause more emotional damage to Michael.

Double Damage Done case studies:

In *The Matrix*, Cypher jumps onto Morpheus and tells everyone Morpheus fed them all bullshit (damages their well-being).

In *Being John Malkovich*, the agent calls the secretary a cunt (emotional damage).

In *Pulp Fiction*, Butch sees someone's gun on the counter (potential damage to his well being).

Minute 88 in *Top Gun*: The enemy blows up Hollywood's plane — Double Damage Done.

MINUTE 89: RED ALERT!

Circumstances grow more serious for hero.

We've all seen that moment in WWII movies where the aircraft carrier's speakers blare out *Red Alert! Red Alert!* as the enemy's torpedo races toward the crippled and vulnerable hull. In a sense, this is what's happening to the hero during this minute....

In *Raiders of the Lost Ark*, Indy holds onto the truck for dear life. There are now six bogeys after the *Top Gun* pilots. In *Star Wars*, Luke and Leia are trapped on the ledge as Stormtroopers fire at them. In *Die Hard*, the distracted Chief makes bogus hostage release calls, which makes the circumstances more serious for John. Julie's father asks "Dorothy" to marry him in *Tootsie*. "He [the Green Goblin] knows who I am," Peter says to himself in *Spider-Man* — Red Alert!

The *Scream* killer grabs Sidney and tries to kill her. In *Little Miss Sunshine*, the stage manager tells woefully ill-prepared Olive that it's time to go onstage. In *The Godfather*, Michael kills the police captain. In *Match Point*, Chris knocks on Nola's neighbor's apartment door — he plans to kill her.

And how do the circumstances grow to Red Alert status in the case studies?

In *The Matrix*, Cypher kills Apoc and Switch, and heads toward Neo to kill him as well. (RED ALERT!)

In *Being John Malkovich*, Lotte and Dr. Lester watch Craig take over Malkovich. (RED ALERT!)

In *Pulp Fiction*, Vincent the hit man steps out of Butch's bathroom. (RED ALERT!)

MINUTE 90: RESCUING ALLY

And just when things have gone *Red Alert!* for the hero, the ally comes to the rescue! Let's see how the ally comes to the rescue in our movie examples:

In *Raiders of the Lost Ark*, Sallah helps Indy and Marion escape.

Iceman and Maverick help each other fight the bogeys. Debbie tells Alison she's young and beautiful in *Knocked Up*. "I would never think you're a freak," Mom tells Cole in *The Sixth Sense*. In *Scream*, Randy tries to help Sidney.

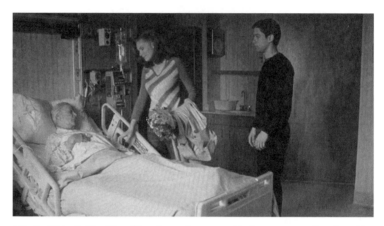

Minute 90 in *Spider-Man*: Mary Jane shows up with flowers to comfort Aunt May — The Rescuing Ally.

In *Forrest Gump*, Lt. Dan helps Forrest on his shrimp boat. The family supports Olive while she performs in *Little Miss Sunshine*. In *Match Point*, the neighbor opens her door to Chris, which helps him with his dark plan. In *Star Wars*, Chewbacca helps Han blast away at the Stormtroopers. In *Die Hard*, the FBI shows up to help.

Who's the Rescuing Ally in our case studies?

In *The Matrix*, Tank helps Trinity return to the Nebuchadnezzar.

In *Being John Malkovich*, other actors show up to support Malkovich's puppetry career.

In *Pulp Fiction*, the tissue (ally in this case) helps Butch hide his fingerprints on the gun.

EXERCISE NINE

Let's find Minute 83's GOTTA GO! moment. After Alabama (Patricia Arquette) beats the dead hitman with the shotgun in Tony Scott's *True Romance*, who grabs her and says, "We gotta go!"? In Ron Howard's *Apollo 13*, why does Jack (Kevin Bacon) hurry to Jim and Fred (Tom Hanks and Bill Paxton)? (Minute 83 starts after Fred shivers and says, "I think Swigert gave me the clap.")

MINUTE 91: SUFFER THE WEAK

When we see that someone we care about is suffering, or they gain the courage to tell you their weakness, we pity or sympathize with them. We've all had those moments of suffering and weakness and can relate. So it is with the characters we've been watching on the screen....

Minute 91 in *Star Wars*: Darth says to Obi-Wan, "Your powers are weak, old man" — Suffer The Weak.

Randy moans from his gunshot wound in *Scream*. In *Spider-Man*, Peter tells Mary Jane he feels stronger and weaker at the same time. In *Raiders of the Lost Ark*, Indy winces in pain. In *Jaws*, Quint says his friend was bit in half by a shark (he suffers from the memory). In *Top Gun*, Maverick says, "It's no good," and pulls out (expressing his weakness). In *The Sixth Sense*, Cole's mom suffers from the memory that her mother never got to see her dance.

In *The Godfather*, the ambulance brings the wounded Don Corleone home. In *Little Miss Sunshine*, pain fills Sheryl and Richard's faces over Olive's performance. Debbie and Alison suffer over their predicament in *Knocked Up*. Forrest and Lt. Dan suffer because they can't find any shrimp. In *Die Hard*, Hans pretends to be weak and helpless.

And how is Suffer The Weak expressed in our remaining case studies?

In *The Matrix*, Agent Smith explains that humans need to suffer.

In *Being John Malkovich*, Craig (as Malkovich) suffers when a student fails to perform puppetry correctly.

In *Pulp Fiction*, Butch slinks toward his car, still not fully confident he is safe.

MINUTE 92: HUGS & KISSES

Hero and ally/love interest show affection.

The hero and ally have been through hell the last fifteen minutes, and as a result they've grown closer and will show affection toward each other in the next two minutes, that's why I call it Hugs & Kisses. It's only natural for them. This moment is also a little breather for the audience as well. But don't let the audience get too comfortable in the lovely-dovey feelings — this is just the calm before the storm....

In *Spider-Man*, Mary Jane holds Peter's hand. In *Raiders of the Lost Ark*, Marion kisses Indy's elbow. In *Jaws*, Quint sings with Hooper and Brody. In *Top Gun*, the pilots show appreciation for Maverick's help. In *The Sixth Sense*, Grandma shows affection for her daughter through Cole's story. In *The Godfather*, Don Corleone and his family show affection for each other. Ben and Pete show brotherly affection in the hotel room in *Knocked Up*. In *Star Wars*, Han, Leia and Luke joke around while planning their next move. In *Die Hard*, John shows affection to Hans (who he thinks is a good guy).

Case study Hugs & Kisses:

In *The Matrix*, Tank, Trinity and Neo try to find a way to save Morpheus (their way of expressing affection for him).

In *Being John Malkovich*, Maxine shows affection toward puppet-Lotte.

In *Pulp Fiction*, Butch merrily sings along with the radio (his ally in this case).

Minute 92 in *Little Miss Sunshine*: Showing their support, the family stands and claps for Olive — Hugs & Kisses.

MINUTE 93: HUGS & KISSES 2

Hero and ally express even greater affection.

The hero and ally connect even more....

In *Spider-Man*, Osborn shows affection toward his son. In *Jaws*, Quint, Brody and Hooper smile and laugh while they sing. In *Top Gun*, Maverick says he's "not leaving without my wing-man." In *The Sixth Sense*, Malcolm sits beside the sleeping Anna and talks lovingly to her. In *The Godfather*, the women cook for the family. In *Knocked Up*, Ben and Pete engage in honest guy talk. In *Star Wars*, Obi-Wan sacrifices his life for Luke. In *Forrest Gump*, Forrest and Lt. Dan smile at each other after catching tons of shrimp. In *Die Hard*, John offers Hans a cigarette. The bomber, pretending to be a good cop, expresses affection toward Annie in *Speed*.

Minute 93 in *Raiders of the Lost Ark* – Hugs & Kisses 2.

And how is Hugs & Kisses 2 expressed in our case studies?

In *The Matrix*, Tank and Trinity want to pull Morpheus's plug so they can save Zion (their way of expressing great affection for Morpheus and his cause).

In *Being John Malkovich*, Craig (as Malkovich) talks lovingly to Maxine.

In *Pulp Fiction*, a witness puts ice on Butch's cut nose.

MINUTE 94: THE AGGRESSOR

Hero or bad guy shows aggression.

As mentioned earlier, we gave the hero and the ally — and the audience — an emotional breather for a couple of minutes. But now the action kicks in again as the bad guy shows aggression....

In *Jaws*, the shark strikes the boat. In *Spider-Man*, Green Goblin belts out an aggressive scream. In *Raiders of the Lost Ark*, something supernatural burns away the Nazi symbol. In *Top Gun*, another enemy bogey appears behind them. Stuart points a gun at Sidney in *Scream*. In *Match Point*, Chris kicks the table. In *Tootsie*, Sandy demands to be let in. The pageant coordinators order the family off the stage in *Little Miss Sunshine*.

In *The Godfather*, Sonny and Tom tell Don Corleone about the hits that have been put out. Ben tells Pete he's a disgusting bitch in *Knocked Up*. In *Forrest Gump*, the people who listen to Forrest's story don't believe him (showing mild aggression). In *Die Hard*, Hans lies to John. In *Speed*, Jack yells at the bad guy to turn around.

Case study aggression:

In *The Matrix*, Neo yells STOP!

In *Being John Malkovich*, Maxine ignores Craig (inside Malkovich).

In *Pulp Fiction*, Butch punches Marsellus and the shop owner points a shotgun at Butch.

MINUTE 95: THE SEPARATION

Hero and ally separate.

Using The Separation is another trick the writer has up their coffee-stained sleeve. Separation creates a longing because we immediately desire for the separated to be reunited. It's an unresolved issue that must be followed up on somehow....

Minute 95 in *Spider-Man*: Peter leaves wounded Aunt May to make a quick call — The Separation.

In *Raiders of the Lost Ark*, Nazis kidnap Marion, separating her from Indy. In *Jaws*, Brody, Quint and Hooper separate to battle the shark. In *Top Gun*, Maverick slows down, which widens the distance between himself and Iceman. In *The Sixth Sense*, Malcolm backpedals away from Anna. In *Scream*, Sidney and Billy (her former ally) separate temporarily.

In *The Godfather*, Don Corleone waves away Tom and Sonny, who leave his bedside. In *Match Point*, Chris moves away from the neighbor's body. In *Knocked Up*, Debbie and Pete separate to do their different party duties. In *Forrest Gump*, Forrest separates from Lt. Dan to go see Mama Gump. In *Die Hard*, John runs away from Hans, who he thought was an ally. Jeff leaves

Michael to go to the other room in *Tootsie*. In *Star Wars*, Luke and Han separate to go to different gun turrets.

And how do our case studies separate?

In *The Matrix*, Neo insists he has to leave his allies.

In *Being John Malkovich*, Craig discovers that Maxine is gone.

In *Pulp Fiction*, Butch passes out (he and his consciousness — his ally in this case — separate).

MINUTE 96: DEATH & DYING

Showing or speaking about death always grabs attention, that's why it's used a few times during a movie. Why? Death & Dying is primal. Death threatens our very existence. Death supercharges our "fight or flight" response....

PHYSICAL THREAT OF DEATH
Billy stabs Stuart in *Scream*. Luke and Han kill the enemy in *Star Wars*. John kills a bad guy in *Die Hard*. Maverick kills the enemy pilot in *Top Gun*. Mary Jane might fall to her death in S*pider-Man*. The barrel pops up — the deadly shark has returned in *Jaws*. In *The Sixth Sense*, Malcolm starts to realize he's dead. The *Little Miss Sunshine* family sees the sheet their dead grandfather was wrapped in. In *Match Point*, Chris waits for Nola with the shotgun.

SPEAKING OF DEATH
In *Raiders of the Lost Ark*, the Captain tells the Nazis he killed Indy. In *The Godfather*, Sonny says, "I'm gonna end it by killing that old bastard." In *Forrest Gump*, Forrest and Mama Gump talk about her dying. In *Speed*, the bomber says he'll blow them up.

How is death shown or spoken about in our case studies?

In *The Matrix*, Neo and Trinity prepare to leave on a deadly mission.

In *Being John Malkovich*, the kidnappers threaten Maxine's life.

In *Pulp Fiction*, the shop owner says to Butch and Marsellus, "Nobody kills people in my place of business except me and Zed."

MINUTE 97:
TAPING THE KNUCKLES

Hero prepares for, or heads toward, the battlefield.

Football players strap on their helmets… boxers tape their knuckles… soldiers load their rifles as they prep for the battle place. Anticipation fills the air as the hero prepares himself for the Big Show.…

For example, Quint, Hooper and Brody rush to pull the barrel out of the water (to prepare for the final battle with the shark) in *Jaws*. Maverick walks toward Iceman for a final verbal battle in *Top Gun*. Malcolm says goodbye to Anna (he prepares to leave her — his final battle) in *The Sixth Sense*. In *Scream*, Sidney prepares for her death. In *Raiders of the Lost Ark*, Indy heads toward the island on the Nazi sub (where his final battle will be).

In *Spider-Man*, Spidey shows up to fight Green Goblin (final battle). Richard prepares to crash through the guard rail (the family's final battle in *Little Miss Sunshine*). In *The Godfather*, Michael prepares to become Don. In *Match Point*, Chris goes into the stairwell to wait for Nola (he prepares, mentally, to shoot her).

In *Star Wars*, Luke, Han, Chewbacca and Leia head back to the rebel hideout to prepare for an attack. In *Forrest Gump*, Mama Gump prepares Forrest for her death. In *Die Hard*, John prepares for the gunfight. Jack runs toward his final battle place with the bomber in *Speed*.

How do our heroes Tape Their Knuckles in our case studies?

In *Being John Malkovich*, Lotte heads toward Maxine with a gun.

In *Pulp Fiction*, Butch prepares to deal with the rapist hillbilly cop.

Minute 97: Neo and Trinity prepare to head back into *The Matrix* for the final battle with the agents — Taping the Knuckles.

MINUTE 98: KISS OR SPIT

Hero or bad guy shows aggression/affection.

The story can go two different ways during the next three minutes. If the movie is ending here on an upbeat note, the hero shows Affection (KISS). If not, Aggression is shown (SPIT), which continues the story in most cases.

AGGRESSION SHOWN

In *Spider-Man*, Green Goblin holds Mary Jane over the scaffolding (SPIT). In *Raiders of the Lost Ark*, Indy beats up the German soldier (SPIT). In *Jaws*, the shark returns to eat Brody, Quint and Hooper (SPIT). In *Scream*, Billy points the gun at Gale (SPIT). In *Knocked Up*, Ben yells at Pete for telling Debbie about doing mushrooms (SPIT). In *Star Wars*, Han and Luke show jealousy toward each other over Leia (SPIT). In *Die Hard*, the bad guys keep looking for John (SPIT). In *Tootsie*, Sandy tells "Dorothy" not to call her (SPIT).

AFFECTION SHOWN

In *The Sixth Sense*, Malcolm tells Anna to "Sleep now, everything will be different in the morning" (KISS). Chris talks tenderly to Chloe over the phone in *Match Point* (KISS). In *Forrest Gump*, the woman stays to listen to Forrest's story (KISS).

Minute 98 in *Top Gun*: "Bullshit, you can be my wingman," Maverick jokes with Iceman (KISS).

Do our case studies Kiss or Spit?

In *The Matrix*, Trinity and Neo head toward the enemy with guns (SPIT).

In *Being John Malkovich*, Lotte shoots the gun and follows a running Maxine into the portal (SPIT).

In *Pulp Fiction*, Zed and the shop owner bring out The Gimp (SPIT).

MINUTE 99: KISS OR SPIT 2

Hero or bad guy shows even more aggression/affection.

AGGRESSION SHOWN

In *Spider-Man*, Green Goblin drops Mary Jane (SPIT). In *Raiders of the Lost Ark*, Indy beats up a soldier and steals his clothes (SPIT). In *Jaws*, the crew follows the shark to kill it (SPIT). In *Scream*, Billy threatens Stuart and Sidney threatens Billy (SPIT). In *Die Hard*, Karl slams his gun in anger (SPIT). In *Tootsie*, Michael's agent yells at him (SPIT). In *Speed*, the bomber threatens Annie even more (SPIT).

Minute 99 in *Knocked Up*: Ben says, "You screwed me, Dad! You gave me terrible advice!" (SPIT).

AFFECTION SHOWN

In *Top Gun*, the Chief shakes Maverick's hand and smiles (KISS). In *The Sixth Sense*, Malcolm kisses Anna in the wedding video. [*The Sixth Sense* ends here.] In *The Godfather*, Michael looks at a Sicilian girl with great affection (KISS). Chris and Chloe watch the opera together in *Match Point* (KISS). In *Forrest Gump*, Forrest shows affection to Bubba's mother by giving her money (KISS).

Case studies:

In *The Matrix*, Agent Smith tells Morpheus he hates this place (SPIT).

In *Being John Malkovich*, Lotte chases Maxine and shoots at her (SPIT).

In *Pulp Fiction*, they take Marsellus into the back room to rape him (SPIT).

During Minute 99 in *Star Wars*, Leia hugs the rebel leader (KISS).

MINUTE 100: KISS OR SPIT 3

Hero and/or bad guy show even greater aggression/affection.

AGGRESSION SHOWN

In *Raiders of the Lost Ark*, Indy purposely bumps into Belloq (SPIT). In *Jaws*, Brody shoots the shark (SPIT). In *Scream*, Billy wants to stab Sidney; Sidney stabs Billy with the umbrella (SPIT). In *Knocked Up*, Ben and Alison refuse to speak to each other (SPIT). In *Star Wars*, the rebels plan their attack on the Death Star (SPIT). Julie rejects "Dorothy's" present in *Tootsie* (SPIT). In *Speed*, the bomber fires his gun at Jack (SPIT).

Minute 100 in *Spider-Man*: Green Goblin attacks Spidey (SPIT).

AFFECTION SHOWN

In *Top Gun*, Charlotte plays "You've Lost That Lovin' Feelin'" for Maverick (KISS). In *The Godfather*, Michael and his companions have a friendly chat with the restaurant owner (KISS). In *Forrest Gump*, Forrest thinks fondly of Jenny (KISS). In *Die Hard*, John and Sgt. Al joke over the walkie-talkie (KISS).

Case studies:

In *The Matrix*, Neo and Trinity shoot the security guards (SPIT).

In *Being John Malkovich*, Lotte yells at Maxine (SPIT).

In *Pulp Fiction*, Butch knocks out The Gimp (SPIT).

EXERCISE TEN

Minute 98 — KISS OR SPIT. How does Rick (Humphrey Bogart) show affection (KISS) in Michael Curtiz's *Casablanca*? Minute 98 begins at the airport when he says, "She tried everything to get them and nothing worked." In David Fincher's *Fight Club*, the minute starts when the guys are driving in the car in the rain. How does Tyler (Brad Pitt) show aggression (SPIT) toward Edward Norton's character?"

EXTENDIN' THE ENDIN'

MINUTE 101: DEEPER DEEPER

There are five ways the hero goes deeper into the story during Minute 101, which we'll examine below. I call it Deeper Deeper because the deeper he goes, the deeper into trouble he gets. The deeper into trouble he gets, the more the audience bites their nails to see how he'll get out of it.

DEEPER INTO BATTLE/TROUBLE

In *Raiders of the Lost Ark,* Indy follows the Nazis deeper into the mountains. In *Jaws,* the shark pulls the crew further out to sea. In *Speed,* Jack goes deeper into the subway tunnel. In *Star Wars,* Luke says he can hit the small target (deepening his commitment to the battle).

Minute 101 in *The Matrix*: Neo and Trinity continue to walk deeper into the protected building — Deeper Deeper.

DEEPER INTO LOVE

In *Top Gun,* Maverick smiles at Charlotte as they fall deeper in love. [*Top Gun* ends here.] In *The Godfather,* Michael orders his companion to get the girl's father (deeper into a relationship with her). In *Forrest Gump,* Jenny returns to Forrest (deeper into a relationship with him). In *Tootsie,* Michael attempts a deeper relationship with Julie.

DEEPER INTO DECEPTION
In *Match Point*, when Chloe sees the newspaper article about Nola's death, Chris pretends like he's shocked.

DEEPER INTO RESPONSIBILITY
In *Knocked Up*, Ben gets his own apartment and decorates the baby's room.

DEEPER INTO FRIENDSHIP
In *Die Hard*, John deepens his friendship with Sgt. Al by listening to his story of how he accidentally shot a kid.

How do the case studies go Deeper Deeper?

In *Being John Malkovich*, Craig stays inside Malkovich, getting DEEPER INTO TROUBLE.

In *Pulp Fiction*, Butch decides to stay and help Marsellus (DEEPER INTO TROUBLE).

MINUTE 102: THE BLOW-UP

And there's bound to be a Blow-Up the deeper into enemy territory the hero goes. The bad guy feels threatened and retaliates. It's inevitable. Nothing like a physical or emotional BLAST to jar the audience too, which is Minute 102's purpose....

Minute 102 in *Spider-Man*: Green Goblin's bomb blows off Spidey's mask – The Blow-Up.

PHYSICAL BLOW UP

In *Raiders of the Lost Ark*, Indy threatens to *blow* up the ark. In *Scream*, Gale Weather's shoots Billy, *blowing* apart his chest. When the shark yanks the rope in *Jaws*, Hooper's thighs take a tremendous *blow*.

EMOTIONAL BLOW UP

In *Forrest Gump*, Jenny's world is *blown* apart when she sees her father's house. In *Star Wars*, Luke and Han's friendship disintegrates (*blows* apart). In *Die Hard*, the FBI agent yells at the cop. In *Tootsie*, Julie closes the door on Michael (*blowing* apart their friendship).

What's The Blow-Up in our case studies?

In *The Matrix*, Neo and Trinity keep blasting away at the enemy, *blowing* apart their bodies.

In *Being John Malkovich*, Craig leaves Malkovich — his coveted time as Malkovich has been *blown* to bits.

In *Pulp Fiction*, Butch descends the basement steps (*blowing* apart his fear).

MINUTE 103: THE BLOW

Hero or bad guy administers some sort of blow.

Another Blow follows the previous minute's blast. The one-two punch, as it were. Again, this can be a physical Blow or and emotional Blow.

PHYSICAL BLOW

In *Spider-Man*, Green Goblin strikes Spidey hard with his foot. In *Jaws*, Hooper almost takes a blow to the head as a barrel zips by. In *Scream*, Sidney shoots Billy in the head [*Scream* **ends here.**] In *Knocked Up*, the baby kicks Alison hard. In *Forrest Gump*, Jenny throws rocks her at father's house (a blow to her father's memory). In *Die Hard*, the FBI shuts down the electricity, a blow to the bad guys' plan.

EMOTIONAL BLOW

In *Raiders of the Lost Ark*, Belloq tells Indy to "go ahead and blow it up" (a blow to Indy's archeological good sense). In *Die Hard*, Hans says he's not going to help the cause (an emotional blow to Luke). In *Tootsie*, Michael goes on a rant, a blow to the director, actors, and producer.

What sort of Blow is administered in our case studies?

In *The Matrix*, Neo and Trinity engage their bomb to blow up the building (PHYSICAL BLOW).

In *Being John Malkovich*, Malkovich shakes violently as old people enter him (PHYSICAL BLOW).

In *Pulp Fiction*, Butch slices the shop owner with the sword (PHYSICAL BLOW).

MINUTE 104: THE UPPER HAND

Hero or bad guy gets the upper hand in an aggressive manner.

The phrase "The Upper Hand" evolved when kids gathered to pick sides for sandlot baseball games. To decide who chose first, one team captain would toss the other captain a baseball bat. The two captains then took turns gripping the bat one fist over the other until there was no more room at the top. The last one to fully grip the bat's handle had control, or "The Upper Hand." The hero and the bad guy play this same game during this minute, but for much higher stakes.

HERO GETS THE UPPER HAND

In *Spider-Man*, Spidey beats up Green Goblin. In *The Godfather*, Michael gives Apollonia a present and wins her over.

BAD GUYS GET THE UPPER HAND

In *Die Hard*, the bad guys break into the vault. In *Raiders of the Lost Ark*, Nazis tie Indy and Marion to the post. In *Match Point*, the detective wants to see Chris. In *Knocked Up*, Ben's friends (bad guys) try to get him out to the club. In *Forrest Gump*, Jenny's awful-father memory gets the better of her. In *Tootsie*, the director yells at his cameramen. In *Speed*, the subway pole won't break and Annie's handcuffed to it.

Minute 104 in *Jaws*: The shark pulls the crew out to sea, getting The Upper Hand.

Who gets The Upper Hand in the case studies?

In *The Matrix*, Neo and Trinity blow up the elevator shaft.

In *Being John Malkovich*, Maxine and Lotte leave Craig and say "Fuck you!"

In *Pulp Fiction*, Butch gets the upper hand on the unarmed Zed; Marsellus shoots Zed.

MINUTE 105: THE DECEIT

Deceit works well three ways. If it is against the hero, we hold our breath and anticipate what's going to happen next; if it's against the bad guy, we cheer; if it's against us, the audience, we silently applaud the storyteller for getting one over on us....

DECEIT AGAINST THE HERO

In *Spider-Man*, Green Goblin *deceives* Spidey by silently flying his ship behind him. In *Jaws*, the shark takes three barrels underneath the water (to *deceive* the crew on where he is). In *Knocked Up*, the doctor has *deceived* Alison — he's not going to be there for the birth. In *Star Wars*, the rebels head out for the secret (*deceptive*) attack. In *Die Hard*, Hans *deceives* the FBI about his real plans.

Minute 105 in *Match Point*: Chris pretends like he had nothing to do with the murder when he talks with the detective — The Deceit.

DECEIT AGAINST THE BAD GUY

In *Raiders of the Lost Ark*, the Nazi reaches his hand into the ark, but clutches only sand (the ark has *deceived* them).

DECEIT AGAINST THE AUDIENCE

In *The Godfather*, we think Michael and Apollonia are walking alone, but then we see bodyguards following them.

What's The Deceit in our case studies?

In *The Matrix*, the helicopter pilot morphs into an agent (DECEIT AGAINST THE HERO).

In *Being John Malkovich*, Dr. Lester hides inside Malkovich while talking to Charlie (DECEIT AGAINST THE HERO).

In *Pulp Fiction*, Marsellus tells Butch not to tell anyone about the rape (DECEIT AGAINST THE BAD GUYS).

MINUTE 106: THE DODGE

Someone dodges or avoids something.

When the hero or ally has to dodge or avoid something bad, we wince for them. It makes us almost want to scream, "Watch out!" (I've actually heard people screaming *look out* during The Dodge moment in theaters). The dilemma keeps us emotionally invested.

In *Spider-Man*, Spidey *dodges* Green Goblin's blades. In *Raiders of the Lost Ark*, Nazi soldiers run away from the ark to *avoid* harm. In *Jaws*, Quint heads toward shallow water to *avoid* being dragged out further. In *The Godfather*, Connie *avoids* showing Sonny her battered face. In *Match Point*, Chris *dodges* the detective's questions over the phone. In *Star Wars*, the rebels *dodge* enemy fire. In *Forrest Gump*, Jenny *avoids* talking about marriage. In *Die Hard*, John resists crying (*avoids* tears). In *Tootsie*, Michael *avoids* being hit. In *Speed*, Jack and Annie *dodge* death as the subway crashes into passing objects.

What is dodged or avoided in our case studies?

In *The Matrix*, Neo *dodges* bullets.

In *Being John Malkovich*, Maxine and Lotte's daughter *avoids* being tickled. [*Being John Malkovich* **ends here.**]

In *Pulp Fiction*, Butch barely *avoids* getting killed by Marsellus.

MINUTE 107: GOOD DOES BAD

Someone that seems good does bad.

The writer designs Minute 107 to give us a glimpse into the hero or ally's darker side — by showing us that good, can indeed, do bad. Why? The audience needs to know that the hero and his friends can fight fire with fire during the final battle.

In *Tootsie*, Michael pushes a mime. In *Forrest Gump*, Forrest has sex with Jenny. In *Die Hard*, John confesses to being an unsupportive husband. In *Spider-Man*, Harry pulls a gun on Spidey. In *The Godfather*, Sonny beats up his sister's husband who used to be his good friend. In *Match Point*, Chris hurls the evidence into the river. In *Knocked Up*, Ben yells at the Doctor over the phone.

Minute 107 in *Raiders of the Lost Ark*: The angel turns into a demon — Good Does Bad.

How does someone who seems good do bad in our case studies?

In *The Matrix*, Neo kills the agents.

In *Pulp Fiction*, Butch steals Zed's motorcycle.

MINUTE 108: SENSE OF FINALITY

The Sense Of Finality during Minute 108 is used for two reasons. Either to help wrap up the story or a subplot, or to create a sense of impending doom to propel the movie forward....

TO HELP WRAP UP THE STORY OR A SUBPLOT
The ark's lid slams shut after it destroys all the Nazis in *Raiders of the Lost Ark*. Harry and Peter hug at the funeral in *Spider-Man*. Michael gives back the engagement ring in *Tootsie*. Ben breaks all ties with the betraying doctor in *Knocked Up*.

IMPENDING DOOM
In *Jaws*, Quint's boat engine shuts off. In *Match Point*, the detective shows Nola's diary to Chris, which Chris was unaware existed (it looks like the jig is up). In *Star Wars*, the enemy fighters close in; rebels are in serious trouble. In *Forrest Gump*, Forrest stares at Jenny's empty bed after she leaves.

Minute 108 in *Die Hard*: The reporter tells John's caretaker that "this is the last time [John's children] will be able to speak to their parents" — Sense Of Finality.

What's the Sense Of Finality in the remaining case studies?

In *The Matrix*, Trinity, Neo, and Morpheus fly away in the helicopter, job done.

In *Pulp Fiction*, Butch is finished with the Marsellus chapter of his life.

MINUTE 109:
THE EXTRAORDINARY

Something extraordinary is revealed.

Since there was a false sense of finality in the last minute, the writer jumpstarts the story again by revealing something extraordinary. This always causes a bigger question to be raised. And when a bigger question is raised, it needs to be answered somehow.

Minute 109 in *Spider-Man*: Mary Jane tells Peter that she kept thinking about him when she was about to die (extraordinary info that sets up the sequel).

In *Die Hard*, John discovers an extraordinary amount of explosives near the roof. In *Raiders of the Lost Ark*, the government agents reveal that the ark is being kept "in a safe place (extraordinary info)." In *Jaws*, Quint says he is out of ideas, which is an extraordinary thing for the normally confident sharker to say). In *The Godfather*, Michael marries Apollonia (an extraordinary thing for the once-engaged-to-someone-else bachelor to do).

In *Match Point*, Chris is mentioned throughout Nola's diary (extraordinary amount of evidence against him). In *Knocked Up*, Ben tells Alison that the doctor is at a bar mitzvah and not going to make it for the birth (extraordinary information based on what the doctor told them earlier). In *Forrest Gump*, Forrest starts "running and running" and doesn't stop (extraordinary behavior for him).

What is The Extraordinary in our case studies?

Just when Neo and Trinity thought they were safe in *The Matrix*, agents riddle the helicopter with an extraordinary amount of bullets.

In *Pulp Fiction*, Butch tells his girlfriend that "This has been the weirdest fuckin' day of my life" (an extraordinary day for him).

MINUTE 110: STRONG STATEMENT

A Strong Statement is made either visually or, most of the time, verbally. Again, this statement is designed to propel the story forward and get the hero deeper into trouble.

VERBALLY

In *Spider-Man*, Mary Jane tells Peter she loves him. In *Jaws*, Hooper suggests they use the shark cage. In *Match Point*, Chris begs the detective to be discreet about his affair. In *Knocked Up*, Alison says to Ben, "You read the baby books?!" In *Star Wars*, Darth says, "Stay in attack formation." In *Forrest Gump*, the old woman says to Forrest, "So, you just ran…" While holding a gun in *Die Hard*, Hans says to Holly, "Nice to make your acquaintance."

VISUALLY

In *Raiders of the Lost Ark*, the government stacks the ark in a cavernous warehouse — a strong statement that they will keep this information hidden from the public. [*Raiders of the Lost*

Ark **ends here.**] In *The Godfather*, Michael dances with Apollonia, making a strong statement to her family that he loves her. In *Tootsie*, Julie rejects Michael with her glare.

What Strong Statement is made in our case studies?

In *The Matrix*, Tank says Neo is "The One."

In *Pulp Fiction*, Jules tells Brett, "And I will strike down upon thee with great vengeance!"

EXERCISE ELEVEN

Minute 102 — THE BLOW-UP. In Mel Gibson's *Braveheart*, who blows up emotionally after Longshanks tosses the advisor out the window? What does the enraged person do exactly? In Steven Soderbergh's *Erin Brockovich*, who does Erin (Julia Roberts) blow up at after Kurt (Peter Coyote) tells Ed (Albert Finnery) that they don't have a smoking gun?

MINUTE 111:
TURN FOR THE WORSE

Oh no!

Another great way to grab the audience's attention, or to extend the story if you need to, is to have the movie take a Turn For The Worse. It's a problem that has to be solved, which keeps the audience watching until it's resolved. A great way to know you're on track is to add the phrase "*Oh no!*" at the end of your Minute 111's description. If the phrase works then you're probably headed in the right direction....

For instance, in *Match Point*, the detectives say they have to keep investigating the crime — a turn for the worse for Chris. (*Oh no!*) In *Star Wars*, Darth kills a rebel pilot, and two other rebel ships are shot down. (*Oh no!*) In *Forrest Gump*, Forrest's appearance rapidly deteriorates. (*Oh no!*) In *Die Hard*, Karl kicks John really hard. (*Oh no!*) In *Knocked Up*, the mean doctor that Ben and Alison rejected earlier shows up to help them. (*Oh no!*) In *Jaws*, Hooper climbs into the woefully inadequate shark cage (their last resort). (*Oh no!*) In *Spider-Man*, Peter tells Mary Jane he can only be friends with her. (*Oh no!*) [**Spider-Man ends here.**]

Minute 111 in *Tootsie*: Julie ignores Michael — Turn For The Worse.

What takes a turn for the worse in our case studies?

In *The Matrix*, the agents order sentinels to strike the Nebuchadnezzar. (*Oh no!*)

In *Pulp Fiction*, the young guy bursts out of the other room and shoots at Jules and Vincent. (*Oh no!*)

MINUTE 112: CHARGING SHARK

Bad guy takes aggressive action toward hero and ally[s].

From Minute 112 to the end of the movie, the bad guy comes on strong in the form of aggressive action, or, as I prefer to call it: Charging Shark (referring to the shark that rushes toward

Hooper in *Jaws*). We're gonna go through these remaining minutes pretty quickly, so try and keep up. (By the way, the phrase "*Oh no!*" works here, too.)

In *Jaws*, the shark swims toward Hooper. In *Star Wars*, more fighters blast away at rebels. In *Forrest Gump*, reporters chase Forrest. In *Die Hard*, Hans throws Holly onto the floor. In *Tootsie*, Julie shuts down Michael. In *The Godfather*, Tom won't tell Kay where Michael is. In *Match Point*, the detective asks Chris if he has access to a shotgun.

Charging Shark case studies:

In *The Matrix*, the subway bum morphs into Agent Smith. (*Oh no!*)

In *Pulp Fiction*, Jules yells at Vincent. (*Oh no!*)

MINUTE 113: THE CAGE SLAM

Bad guy takes another aggressive action toward hero and ally[s].

The Cage Slam refers to the moment the shark rams his nose into Hooper's fragile cage during this minute in *Jaws*. Here are other ways the bad guys slam into our hero and ally's cages in other movies:

In *Star Wars*, Darth kills another rebel. Tom refuses Kay's letter in *The Godfather*. The detective thinks Chris is involved in the murder in *Match Point*. An annoying man chases Forrest in *Forrest Gump*. Hans yells at Holly in *Die Hard*. Julie glares at Michael in *Tootsie*.

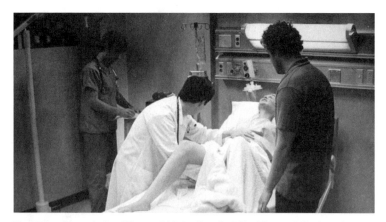

The Cage Slam during Minute 113 in *Knocked Up*: The umbilical cord wraps around the baby's neck.

Case Studies:

In *The Matrix*, Agent Smith shoots the phone, forcing Neo to stay.

In *Pulp Fiction*, Vincent argues with Jules.

MINUTE 114: GETS THE BETTER

Bad guy gets the better of hero and/or ally.

We think the hero might have a chance, but then the bad guy Gets The Better of them, which increases the audience's anxiety.

The shark eats through Hooper's cage in *Jaws*. Connie's husband yells at her in *The Godfather*. Paranoia overwhelms Chris in *Match Point*. The mean doctor yells at Ben and Alison in *Knocked Up*. The Death Star blasts away at Luke in *Star Wars*. The bad guys take hostages up to the bombed-rigged roof in *Die Hard*.

How does the bad guy Get The Better of the hero or ally in the case study?

In *The Matrix*, during the fight, Agent Smith gets the better of Neo.

In *Pulp Fiction*, the blood all over Jules and Vincent could get them arrested.

MINUTE 115: BLEAK MEEK

It looks like the suddenly passive hero (meek) might be defeated after all (bleak). That's why I call this minute Bleak Meek. Let's see how this plays out in our movie examples:

In *Die Hard*, the FBI shoots at John during Minute 115. John runs away (meek) before the enemy kills him (bleak).

In *Jaws*, defeated Quint and Brody (*meek*) pull up the mutilated cage — Hooper's not in it (*bleak*). In *The Godfather*, Connie's husband beats her (*meek*) with a strap (*bleak*). (*Meek*) Chris gets even more paranoid (*bleak*) in *Match Point*. Luke's wingman pulls out (*meek*) and Darth closes in (*bleak*) in *Star Wars*. Forrest has nowhere else to turn (*meek*); he's completely by himself (*bleak*) in *Forrest Gump*.

How does it look bleak for the meek hero in the case studies?

In *The Matrix*, Agent Smith punches Neo (*meek*) hard and he bleeds (*bleak*) in the real world.

In *Pulp Fiction*, Jules and Vincent are in serious trouble (*meek*) because of the blood and dead body (*bleak*).

MINUTE 116:
KICK 'EM WHILE THEY'RE DOWN

Bad guy exerts tremendous effort against hero.

The bad guy sees that the hero is hurt, so he's going to Kick 'Em While He's Down to make sure he doesn't rise back up.

Hans blows up the roof in *Die Hard*. Darth closes in on Luke in *Star Wars*. Connie's husband beats her even more in *The Godfather*. Nola's ghost appears to paranoid Chris in *Match Point*. Alison is having extreme difficulty giving birth in *Knocked Up*. In *Forrest Gump*, someone shoots President Reagan.

Minute 116 in *Jaws*: The shark leaps onto the boat — Kick 'Em While They're Down.

How does the bad guy Kick 'Em While He's Down in the case studies?

In *The Matrix*, Agent Smith punches Neo's stomach with incredible speed.

In *Pulp Fiction*, Jimmy yells at Jules for bringing a dead body to his house.

MINUTE 117: REPRIEVE

Yes, *but…*

Yes, it does look really bad for the hero during this minute, but he does something that might give him a glimmer of hope, which is why I call this moment The Reprieve….

Jaws: Yes, the shark swims toward Brody, *but* Brody shoves an air canister into its mouth. *Match Point*: Yes, Nola's ghost tells Chris he'll be sought out, *but* he argues against it. *Knocked Up*: Yes, Debbie tells Ben he can leave now, *but* he refuses. *Forrest Gump*: Yes, it does seem uncomfortable between Jenny and Forrest, *but* Forrest eases the discomfort by giving Jenny a present. *Die Hard*: Yes, it looks like John is going to fall to his death, *but* he crashes safely through a window instead. *The Godfather*: Yes, the enemy riddles Sonny's car with bullets, *but* he opens the door and tries to escape.

The Reprieve during Minute 117 in *Star Wars*: Yes, things look really bleak for the rebels, *but* Luke decides to fire at the target anyway.

Case studies:

The Matrix: Yes, Agent Smith shows the wounded Neo the train that's going to kill him, *but* Neo leaps out of the way.

Pulp Fiction: Yes, it looks like Jimmy's wife might come home and see the body, *but* Jules figures out a possible solution — he'll call someone who can help get rid of it.

MINUTE 118: HOPE MIGHT BE LOST

Nope, forget that glimmer of hope in the last minute. Hope Might Be Lost for good during Minute 118 as the bad guy hurts the hero, or ally, even more....

In *Jaws*, the boat tilts and sinks as the shark closes in on Brody. In *The Godfather*, Sonny is dead (all hope might be lost for the Corleone family). In *Star Wars*, R2-D2 looks permanently damaged. In *Knocked Up*, Ben tells Debbie to "back the fuck off" (hope might be lost for their friendship). It doesn't look good for injured John in *Die Hard*.

Minute 118 in *Match Point*: The detective bolts upright in bed, convinced that Chris Wilton did it — Hope Might Be Lost for Chris.

How might hope be lost in the case studies?

In *The Matrix*, the Sentinels are coming! Pedestrians morph into agents and blast away at Neo.

In *Pulp Fiction*, Bonnie will soon be home! They have to get the body out of Jimmy's house ASAP!

MINUTE 119: ONE BULLET LEFT

Hero fails, or needs help, as the bad guy closes in.

It's never easy, is it? So it is for our hero who goes to meet the bad guy with only One Bullet Left in his chamber, either literally or emotionally.

In *Jaws*, Brody shoots, but fails to hit the air canister. In *The Godfather*, Tom needs a drink to gain the courage to tell Don Corleone that his son is dead. In *Forrest Gump*, guilt overcomes Forrest when Jenny tells him he's a father.

Minute 119 in *Die Hard*: John is (nearly) out of bullets as he approaches Hans — One Bullet Left.

One Bullet Left case studies:

In *The Matrix*, Neo fails to defeat Agent Smith.

In *Pulp Fiction*, Jules needs help from Marsellus before Bonnie returns.

MINUTE 120: POWDER KEG

Minute 120 is the Power Keg that will, or finally does, blow. And it comes in the form of a physical or emotional explosion. And this explosion is much more intense than the previous explosions.

PHYSICAL EXPLOSION

In *Knocked Up*, Alison *screams* in pain. In *Die Hard*, Argyle *crashes* into the bad guy's van.

EMOTIONAL EXPLOSION

In *The Godfather*, Don Corleone breaks into tears over his son's death. In *Match Point*, Chloe gives birth to Chris's baby (an *explosive* moment in Chris's life). An *explosion* of cheers erupts for Luke, Han and Chewbacca in *Star Wars*. In *Forrest Gump*, Forrest cries because he has a son.

Minute 120 in *Jaws*: The shark explodes – The Powder Keg.

And what is the Powder Keg in our remaining case studies?

In *The Matrix*, Morpheus prepares the *explosives* (for a PHYSICAL EXPLOSION).

In *Pulp Fiction*, the situation comes to a head — they *have* to get the body out before Bonnie gets home and freaks out (EMOTIONAL EXPLOSION).

EXERCISE TWELVE

During Minute 118 — HOPE MIGHT BE LOST. How might hope be lost for Woodward and Bernstein in Alan J. Pakula's *All The President's Men*? Start your stopwatch when all the reporters are gathered together and Harry (Jack Warden) says, "We're not a bunch of zanies about to bring it down!" In Ridley Scott's *Thelma & Louise*, what do the girls see that indicates HOPE MIGHT BE LOST? Start your stopwatch when Thelma (Geena Davis) drives the car through the wooden gate.

THAT'S A WRAP

I appreciate your taking the time to read my book. I hope it has deepened your understanding into movie stories and has elevated your writing, directing, producing, acting, or editing. Can't wait to see your movies on the big screen! Please let me know when they are in development and how *Something Startling Happens* has helped you. It's why I wrote the book — to help make that happen for you. You can contact me through my website, *writerwrench.com*. I developed the site for you — it combines over a decade's worth of the world's best story fix-it links into one, easy-to-navigate site. Industry friends and I use it all the time. And please sign up for *Writer Wrench Weekly* while you're there. I think you'll enjoy the continued industry insights and updates on *Something Startling Happens*.

See you at the coffeeshop!

Todd Klick
Santa Monica, CA

EXERCISE ANSWERS

EXERCISE ONE
Answer: In *Notting Hill*, William sees Anna's face for the first time, which is the JAW DROPPER for him because she is a world-famous actress. In *Wall Street*, Bud's JAW DROPPER happens when he finds out that his boss is going to make him pay for his client's loss.

EXERCISE TWO
Answer: In *Sneakers*, Marty's BIG CONCERN is that he might go to jail if he doesn't take the agents' offer. In *Stand By Me*, the boys' BIG CONCERN is that they forgot to bring food.

EXERCISE THREE
Answer: In *When Harry Met Sally*, THE BIG UNEXPECTED is when Harry tells Jess that his wife is seeing someone else. In *Kill Bill*, THE BIG UNEXPECTED is when The Bride bites the redneck's tongue and he screams.

EXERCISE FOUR
Answer: Amélie shows that she is OVER HER HEAD by crying, and by looking forlorn while she rides the subway alone. In *Titanic*, Rose shows she is OVER HER HEAD by preparing to jump to her death.

EXERCISE FIVE
Answer: In *Up In The Air*, THE THORNY ROSE for Ryan is when he overhears Natalie say, "No, I don't even think of him that way. He's old." In *The Game*, the THE THORNY ROSE moment is when Nicholas and the waitress discover that the elevator doesn't work; in fact, the wiring has been gutted.

EXERCISE SIX

Answer: In *Ghost*, Sam's SIDESWIPE moment is when he learns that his best friend knows his killer. *Total Recall* packs in two SIDESWIPE moments: Melina *sideswipes* Douglas with a slap; then Douglas *sideswipes* her by saying he doesn't remember her.

EXERCISE SEVEN

Answer: In *Unbreakable*, THE POSITIVE STEP is when David plays a fun question/answer game with his wife. In *About a Boy*, Will's POSITIVE STEP is when he confesses, through narration, that he really loves Marcus.

EXERCISE EIGHT

Answer: In *Hannah and Her Sisters*, the THE RUMBLE moment is when Hannah and Holly argue over Holly's job situation and life. In *The Shining*, the argument/fight is about leaving the hotel.

EXERCISE NINE

Answer: In *True Romance*, the GOTTA GO! moment is when Clarence grabs Alabama and says, "Come on, darling. We gotta get the fuck out of here!" In *Apollo 13*, Jack hurries to Jim and Fred and informs them that they might skip right out of the atmosphere and never get back.

EXERCISE TEN

Answer: In *Casablanca*, Rick shows affection (KISS) by telling Victor that Ilsa doesn't love him anymore — Rick's supreme act of self-sacrifice for Ilsa; he then shakes Lazlo's hand, another gesture of affection. In *Fight Club*, Tyler shows aggression (SPIT) by screaming "Let go!" at Edward Norton's character.

EXERCISE ELEVEN

Answer: Enraged (THE BLOW-UP), Longshanks' son tries to stab his father in *Braveheart*. In *Erin Brockovich*, THE BLOW-UP occurs when Erin yells at Ed for not informing her.

EXERCISE TWELVE

Answer: In *All The President's Men*, the HOPE MIGHT BE LOST moment is when Ben tells Woodward and Bernstein that he's "not sure." "Get another source," he says. As a team of cop cars chases Thelma and Louise, they realize HOPE MIGHT BE LOST when they see a concrete bridge (the bridge might stop their escape).

GLOSSARY

Below are the *Something Startling Happens* catch phrases that you can use while: 1) developing your script; 2) working with other writers; 3) using index cards; 4) making a pitch; 5) shooting a scene; 6) producing a script; 7) editing a film; 8) acting in a scene.

AGGRESSOR, THE: The hero or bad guy shows aggression during Minute 94.

ALLY AID: The ally or love interest takes a positive or significant step toward the hero during Minute 68.

ALLY ATTACK: The bad guy, or secondary bad guy, deeply affects the hero's ally or love interest during Minute 63.

ALLY'S WORLD: We learn more about the ally and their world during Minute 40.

ANOTHER NOTCH: Minute 4's catch phrase which builds upon the previous minute's The Ratchet. A good phrase to use here is "If you thought that was bad..." as in: *If you thought that was bad*, now the shark bites the girl and drags her around.

ANXIETY AMP: A sought-after truth or object is revealed and causes great anxiety during Minute 32.

ATTENTION!: How a movie story starts during Minute 1 of a screenplay. Tension grabs attention.

BAD GUY THREAT: The bad guy, or secondary bad guy, threatens the hero in some way during Minute 64.

BAD TO THE BONE: A reference to the George Thorogood song that sums up the bad guy, or secondary bad guy, showing aggression during Minute 71.

BADDER TO THE BONE: A building upon of Minute 71 which is called Bad To The Bone, a reference to the George Thorogood song that sums up the bad guy, or secondary bad guy, showing aggression. Badder to the Bone happens during Minute 72.

BADDEST TO THE BONE: A building upon of Minutes 71 and 72 which are called Bad To The Bone and Badder To The Bone, a reference to the George Thorogood song that sums up the bad guy, or secondary bad guy, showing more aggression. Baddest to the Bone happens during Minute 73.

BAD GUY BOO BOO: Refers to the bad guy getting hurt during Minute 85. It shows that the bad guy is vulnerable and could possibly be defeated.

BAIT & SWITCH: Seems like this new world (that the hero is experiencing in the movie) is positive, but is it really? This happens during Minute 35.

BIG CONCERN, THE: The troubled or anxious state of mind that occurs during Minute 16, that happens to either the hero or ally.

BIG QUEST PREP: Hero prepares for a bigger quest with ally during Minute 28.

BIG QUEST PREP 2: Building upon Minute 28's Big Quest Prep, the hero and/or ally's preparation for the bigger quest continues during Minute 29.

BIG QUEST ONE-EIGHTY: This moment happens around Minute 30 and is the traditional start of Act Two, or where the hero begins his or her Big Quest. This is also when the hero heads into a world that is a complete one-eighty of his normal life.

BIG UNEXPECTED, THE: An unexpected moment during Minute 26 that keeps the hero and the audience off balance.

BLEAK MEEK: Refers to Minute 115 when things look bleak for the meek hero.

BLOW, THE: The hero or bad guy administers some sort of blow during Minute 103.

BLOW-UP, THE: Referring to Minute 102 when something blows up either physically or emotionally.

BUILD, THE: Used during Minute 2 where audience anticipation is built by "building upon" already existing tension. A good phrase to use during this minute is "Not only does," as in: "*Not only does* Casey get a mysterious call from a stranger, but the stranger calls a *third* time."

CAGE SLAM, THE: Refers to Minute 113, when the shark rams his nose into Hooper's cage in *Jaws*.

CAPTIVATING CONCERN: Concern is shown during Minute 69, but with a little more at stake.

CHARGING SHARK: The bad guy takes aggressive action toward the hero and ally during Minute 112.

DAMAGE DONE: The bad guy provokes physical or emotional damage during Minute 87.

DANGER WATCH: A docile hero watches danger approaching during Minute 14.

DARK TWIST CHAT: The hero talks with a friend during Minute 56, and then there's a dark twist.

DEATH & DYING: Refers to the prominence of death and dying being the main feature during Minute 96.

DECEIT, THE: Referring to Minute 105 where some sort of deceit occurs.

DECEPTION, THE: Some form of deception, in words or deed, happens during Minute 59.

DEEPER DEEPER: Referring to Minute 101 where the hero goes deeper into the story.

DIFFICULT WORDS: A difficult question/request/statement is asked or made during Minute 57.

DISCUSSION, THE: Someone important to the hero wants to discuss something significant during Minute 10.

DISTRESS SIGNAL: The hero sees/hears something that distresses him during Minute 31.

DODGE, THE: Someone dodges or avoids something during Minute 106.

DOUBLE DAMAGE DONE: A building upon Minute 87's Damage Done wherein the bad guy causes *additional* physical or emotional damage during Minute 88.

ENGAGE, THE: The hero and/or ally engages the enemy, the enemy intimidates the hero during Minute 51.

ESCORT, THE: The ally takes, or will take, the hero somewhere during Minute 47.

EXTRAORDINARY, THE: Something extraordinary is revealed during Minute 109.

FINAL QUEST: Depending on how long your story is, somewhere between Minutes 80 and 110 is the last push toward the final battle place.

FLIRTIN' WITH DISASTER: A reference to the Molly Hatchet song that also refers to movies flirting with some sort of disaster during Minute 62.

FOREBODING FACT: The hero is given more knowledge/warning, often ominous during Minute 49.

FRIEND AFFECT: Ally's behavior affects the hero during Minute 34, either in words or deeds.

FRIEND OR FIST: The hero and ally bond or fight during Minute 6, which defines their relationship and helps us get to know them better.

FRIEND OR FIST 2: The phrase used to define Minute 7, which builds upon Minute's 6's Bond Or Fight. During this minute the hero and ally bond or fight, which defines their relationship and helps us get to know them better.

GAP SUBTRACT: Gap between hero and bad guy/ally decreases during Minute 84.

GETS THE BETTER: The bad guy gets the better of hero and/or ally during Minute 114.

GOOD DOES BAD: Someone that seems good does bad during Minute 107.

GOTTA GO!: Refers to the hero hurrying off somewhere in Minute 83.

GREAT AFFECT, THE: Something happens during Minute 21 that greatly affects the hero.

GRIM REAPER, THE: A reference to The Grim Reaper, which sums up death making a stronger appearance during Minute 76.

HARSHER WARNING: Building upon Minute 11's The Warning, Minute 12 is where a harsher warning or threat is made.

HERO AFFECT: The hero does something that will immediately or eventually affect the main bad guy during Minute 67.

HIDE & SEEK: The main object of desire stays hidden during Minute 36.

HOPE MIGHT BE LOST: Refers to Minute 118 where it looks like hope might be lost for the hero.

HUGS & KISSES: The hero and ally/love interest show affection during Minute 92.

HUGS & KISSES 2: Builds upon Minute 92's Hugs & Kisses where the hero and ally/love interest show more affection during Minute 93.

INTIMIDATION, THE: The enemy intimidates hero during Minute 53.

JAW DROPPER: A Minute 5 moment that makes the audience's jaw drop. It's where something extraordinary or astonishing happens in a movie.

KICK 'EM WHILE THEY'RE DOWN: The bad guy exerts tremendous effort against hero during Minute 116.

KISS OR SPIT: The hero or bad guy shows either aggression or affection during Minute 98.

KISS OR SPIT 2: A building upon Minute 98's Kiss Or Spit, where the hero or bad guy shows more aggression or affection during Minute 99.

KISS OR SPIT 3: A building upon Minute 98's and 99's Kiss Or Spit, where the hero or bad guy shows even more aggression or affection during Minute 100.

LIGHTBULB, THE: A new positive or negative revelation is made during Minute 54.

MASSIVE MIDPOINT MOMENT: A moment between Minutes 55 and 62 when things get way more serious for the hero. It's a radical event that forces the hero into seeing things through to the bitter end.

MINI-QUEST, THE: During Minute 27, a Mini-Quest happens just before the upcoming Big Quest.

MYSTERY MISSION: Hero and ally interact; there's a mystery that needs to be solved during Minute 78.

MYSTERY MISSION 2: A building upon Minute 78's Mystery Mission where the hero and ally continue to interact; there's a mystery that needs to be solved during Minute 79.

NEED, THE: An overriding need, usually expressed by the hero, is shown or expressed during Minute 30.

NEEDED KNOWLEDGE: The ally gives/shows hero needed knowledge during Minute 48.

NEW JOURNEY: One of the main characters in the movie embark on a new journey during Minute 70.

NEW JOURNEY BOND: The hero bonds further with main ally on new journey during Minute 39.

NEW NEWS: The hero reacts to New News during Minute 44.

OMINOUS OH NO!: The hero sees/does/hears something ominous during Minute 33.

ONE BULLET LEFT: Taken from Minute 119 where both John McClane in *Die Hard* and Chief Brody in *Jaws* both have only one bullet left when they go to meet the bad guy.

OUT OF THE ORDINARY: Hero does something brave and out of the ordinary for him during Minute 45.

OVER HIS HEAD: The hero or ally realizes that he may be in over his head during Minute 37.

PLUS MINUS: A positive turns into a negative, or a negative turns into a positive, during Minute 61.

PORTENT, THE: Something potentially deadly is seen or explained during Minute 50.

POSITIVE RECONNECT: The hero reconnects with ally in a positive way during Minute 38.

POSITIVE STEP: The hero does something positive toward his goal during Minute 66.

POWDER KEG, THE: Refers to Minute 120 when the powder keg of a situation either explodes physically or emotionally.

PURSUIT, THE: The hero discovers something extraordinary or astonishing during Minute 9 that must be pursued.

PUSH BACK: Up until Minute 20 the hero has been pushed around, now it's his turn to push back.

PUT INTO PERIL: The hero and/or ally is put into peril during Minute 74.

RATCHET, THE: Just like a ratchet wrench escalates the tension in the wrist when tightening a bolt, added tension ratchets the story during Minute 3. A good phrase to use here is "Not only that, but..." as in: *Not only that, but now* Morpheus tells Trinity they've been compromised — agents are outside!"

RED ALERT!: Circumstances grow more serious for the hero during Minute 89.

REPRIEVE: Things look really, *really* bleak for the hero during Minute 117, but he does something that might save him.

RESCUING ALLY: Refers to Minute 90, when the ally comes to the hero's rescue.

RESISTANCE, THE: The hero or ally attacks or resists the bad guy during Minute 65.

REVELATION, THE: A revelation during the movie's Minute 46 that comes in four different forms: 1) Revelations that rock the hero's world; 2) Revelations about the ally; 3) Revelations about the hero; 4) Revelations about the bad guy.

RUMBLE, THE: Refers to Minute 77 where some sort of fight breaks out, either physically or emotionally.

SAY UNCLE: The common schoolyard phrase that encapsulates what happens during Minute 52. Not only does the enemy intimidate the hero in the previous minute, now he almost defeats him.

SCARY STUFF: Hero experiences something scary with ally or love interest during Minute 23.

SCARY STUFF 2: Building upon the previous Minute 23, the hero and/or ally/love interest experience *more* scary stuff during Minute 24.

SCARY STUFF 3: Building upon the previous Minutes 23 and 24, the hero and/or ally/love interest experience *even more* scary stuff during Minute 25.

SENSE OF FINALITY: Referring to Minute 108 where either there's a wrap up of the story or a subplot, or there's a sense of impending doom.

SEPARATION, THE: The hero and ally separate during Minute 95.

SHOCKER, THE: Something that draws a swift inhalation of breath from the audience that happens to the hero or his allies during Minute 60.

SIDESWIPE: During Minute 55 there is some kind of surprise — a sideswiping moment — which give the hero and the audience a jolt.

SKULL AND CROSSBONES: Referring to death making an appearance of sum sort during Minute 75.

SOMETHING STARTLING HAPPENS: Something startling happens during Minute 8, usually to the hero.

STRONG STATEMENT: Refers to Minute 110 where a strong statement is made either visually or, most of the time, verbally.

SUBMISSION, THE: A final warning or threat is made and the hero submits during Minute 13.

SUFFER THE WEAK: Some sort of suffering or weakness is expressed during Minute 91.

SURPRISED HERO: The bad guy or ally surprises hero during Minute 81.

SURPRISE REVEAL: During Minute 42 the ally/hero reveals something surprising.

SURPRISE REVEAL 2: Building upon Minute 42's Surprising Reveal, the Ally/Hero reveals something even more surprising during Minute 43.

SURPRISE-SURPRISE: Refers to the second surprise during Minute 82 that follows Minute 81's Surprised Hero.

TAPING THE KNUCKLES: Refers to Minute 97 where the hero prepares for battle.

TICK TICK BOOM: Refers to Minute 80, which is just like a stick of dynamite that finally goes off.

THORNY ROSE: Things may seem kinda rosy, but there's still ugliness out there during Minute 41.

THREAT, THE: The bad guy, or secondary bad guys, make a threat or warning during Minute 19.

TROUBLE TURN: The event during Minute 18 that will get the hero into trouble later.

TRUTH DECLARED: Someone speaks a truth during Minute 22.

TURN FOR THE WORSE: Refers to Minute 111 where the story takes a turn for the worse, usually for the hero. A good phrase to use during this minute is "Oh no!" as in: "Darth kills a rebel pilot, and two other rebel ships are shot down. *Oh no!*"

UPPER HAND, THE: The hero or bad guy gets the upper hand in an aggressive manner during Minute 104.

VITAL EVENT: An event during Minute 58 that either alters the hero's life, touches upon the past, reveals the state of a relationship, or poses a threat.

WARNING, THE: A warning or threat is made during Minute 11.

WHEW, THAT WAS CLOSE!: Hero experiences a close call while danger approaches during Minute 15.

WORLD UPSIDE DOWN: The bad guy turns a good person's world upside down during Minute 17.

WORRY WOUND: Something worries and wounds our characters during Minute 86.

FILMOGRAPHY

About A Boy, 2002, Universal Pictures

Alien, 1979, Twentieth Century-Fox

All The President's Men, 1976, Warner Bros

Amélie, 2001, ZOE Pictures

Apollo 13, 1995, Universal Pictures

Being John Malkovich, 1999, Universal Pictures

Braveheart, 1992, Paramount Pictures

Casablanca, 1942, Warner Bros.

Die Hard, 1988, Twentieth Century-Fox

Erin Brockovich, 2000, Universal

Fight Club, 1999, Twentieth Century-Fox

Forrest Gump, 1994, Paramount Pictures

The Game, 1997, PolyGram Filmed

The Godfather, 1992, Paramount Pictures

Ghost, 1990, Paramount Pictures

Halloween, 1978, Compass International Pictures

Hannah and Her Sisters, 1986, Orion Pictures Corporation

Jaws, 1975, Universal Pictures

Juno, 2007, Fox Searchlight Pictures

Kill Bill, 2003, Miramax Films

Knocked Up, 2007, Universal Pictures

Little Miss Sunshine, 2006, Fox Searchlight Pictures

Match Point, 2005, DreamWorks

The Matrix, 1999, Warner Bros. Pictures

Notting Hill, 1999, Universal Pictures

Pulp Fiction, 1994, Miramax Films

Raiders of the Lost Ark, 1981, Paramount Pictures

Rashomon, 1950, RKO Radio Pictures

Scream, 1996, Dimension Films

The Sixth Sense, 1999, Hollywood Pictures

Sneakers, 1993, Universal Studios

Speed, 1994, Twentieth Century-Fox

Spider-Man, 2002, Columbia Pictures

Stand By Me, 1986, Columbia Pictures

Star Wars, 1977, Twentieth Century-Fox

Thelma & Louise, 1991, Metro-Goldwyn-Mayer

Titanic, 1997, Paramount Pictures

Tootsie, 1982, Columbia Pictures

Top Gun, 1986, Paramount Pictures

Total Recall, 1990, TriStar Pictures

True Romance, 1993, Warner Bros.

Unbreakable, 2000, Touchstone Pictues

Up In The Air, 2009, Paramount Pictures

Wall Street, 1987, Twentieth Century-Fox

ABOUT THE AUTHOR

Screenwriter, producer, and author **TODD KLICK** is VP and Director of Story Development for White Oak Films. Outside of his work with White Oak, Todd (whose screenplays have earned him recognition with the prestigious Nicholl Fellowship and the PAGE International screenplay competitions) currently earned four options for his latest feature-length screenplays and signed a deal with the Hallmark Channel. Todd has appeared on *Dateline NBC*, *NPR*, and *Fox News* to promote his work. He is also the co-founder of the story fix-it website, *writerwrench.com*.

THE MYTH OF MWP

In a dark time, a light bringer came along, leading the curious and the frustrated to clarity and empowerment. It took the well-guarded secrets out of the hands of the few and made them available to all. It spread a spirit of openness and creative freedom, and built a storehouse of knowledge dedicated to the betterment of the arts.

The essence of the Michael Wiese Productions (MWP) is empowering people who have the burning desire to express themselves creatively. We help them realize their dreams by putting the tools in their hands. We demystify the sometimes secretive worlds of screenwriting, directing, acting, producing, film financing, and other media crafts.

By doing so, we hope to bring forth a realization of 'conscious media' which we define as being positively charged, emphasizing hope and affirming positive values like trust, cooperation, self-empowerment, freedom, and love. Grounded in the deep roots of myth, it aims to be healing both for those who make the art and those who encounter it. It hopes to be transformative for people, opening doors to new possibilities and pulling back veils to reveal hidden worlds.

MWP has built a storehouse of knowledge unequaled in the world, for no other publisher has so many titles on the media arts. Please visit www.mwp.com where you will find many free resources and a 25% discount on our books. Sign up and become part of the wider creative community!

Onward and upward,

Michael Wiese
Publisher/Filmmaker

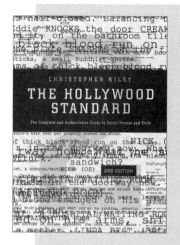

THE HOLLYWOOD STANDARD
2ND EDITION
THE COMPLETE AND AUTHORITATIVE GUIDE TO SCRIPT FORMAT AND STYLE

CHRISTOPHER RILEY

This is the book screenwriter Antwone Fisher (*Antwone Fisher, Tales from the Script*) insists his writing students at UCLA read. This book convinced John August (*Big Fish, Charlie and the Chocolate Factory*) to stop dispensing formatting advice on his popular writing website. His new advice: Consult *The Hollywood Standard*. The book working and aspiring writers keep beside their keyboards and rely on every day. Written by a professional screenwriter whose day job was running the vaunted script shop at Warner Bros., this book is used at USC's School of Cinema, UCLA, and the acclaimed Act One Writing Program in Hollywood, and in screenwriting programs around the world. It is the definitive guide to script format.

The Hollywood Standard describes in clear, vivid prose and hundreds of examples how to format every element of a screenplay or television script. A reference for everyone who writes for the screen, from the novice to the veteran, this is the dictionary of script format, with instructions for formatting everything from the simplest master scene heading to the most complex and challenging musical underwater dream sequence. This new edition includes a quick start guide, plus new chapters on avoiding a dozen deadly formatting mistakes, clarifying the difference between a spec script and production script, and mastering the vital art of proofreading. For the first time, readers will find instructions for formatting instant messages, text messages, email exchanges and caller ID.

"Aspiring writers sometimes wonder why people don't want to read their scripts. Sometimes it's not their story. Sometimes the format distracts. To write a screenplay, you need to learn the science. And this is the best, simplest, easiest to read book to teach you that science. It's the one I recommend to my students at UCLA."

— Antwone Fisher, from the foreword

CHRISTOPHER RILEY is a professional screenwriter working in Hollywood with his wife and writing partner, Kathleen Riley. Together they wrote the 1999 theatrical feature *After the Truth*, a multiple-award-winning German language courtroom thriller. Since then, the husband-wife team has written scripts ranging from legal and political thrillers to action-romances for Touchstone Pictures, Paramount Pictures, Mandalay Television Pictures and Sean Connery's Fountainbridge Films.

In addition to writing, the Rileys train aspiring screenwriters for work in Hollywood and have taught in Los Angeles, Chicago, Washington D.C., New York, and Paris. From 2005 to 2008, the author directed the acclaimed Act One Writing Program in Hollywood.

$24.95 · 208 PAGES · ORDER NUMBER 130RLS · ISBN: 9781932907636

THE COFFEE BREAK SCREENWRITER
WRITING YOUR SCRIPT TEN MINUTES AT A TIME

PILAR ALESSANDRA

BEST SELLER

At last, leading Hollywood screenwriting instructor Pilar Alessandra shows everyone who's ever wanted to write a screenplay how to do it — without quitting their jobs or leaving their families. Packed with over sixty 10-minute writing tools, *The Coffee Break Screenwriter* keeps it focused and keeps it simple. Now, writers can make real progress on their scripts with only ten minutes of stolen time.

The writer receives guidance and tips at every stage of the often intimidating writing process with a relaxed, "ten minutes at a time" method that focuses the writer and pushes him or her forward. At each step, writers are encouraged to "Take Ten" and tackle an element of their scripts using the templates and tools provided. "What You've Accomplished" sections help writers review their progress. And "Ten Minute Lectures" distill and demystify old-school theory, allowing the writer to unblock and keep writing.

"I had a 'first-draft paperweight' on my desk for months. With Pilar's help, my scripts have transformed from desk clutter into calling cards. I've been hired by Warner Bros., signed with ICM, and am a new member of the WGA. I can honestly say that I wouldn't be in the position I am today if it weren't for Pilar."

> — Bill Birch, writer of *Shazam*, Warner Bros.

"Pilar's techniques not only fine-tune your draft but serve as lessons that stick with you and make you a better writer overall. I highly recommend her if you want to take your writing to the next level!"

> — Monica Macer, staff writer *Prison Break* and *Lost*; former creative executive Disney Studios

PILAR ALESSANDRA is the director of the Los Angeles writing program "On the Page," which has helped thousands of screenwriters write and develop their feature and television scripts. She's worked as Senior Story Analyst for DreamWorks and Radar Pictures and has trained writers at ABC/Disney, MTV/Nickelodeon, the National Screen Institute, the Los Angeles Film School, The UCLA Writers Program, and more. Her students and clients have sold to Disney, DreamWorks, Warner Brothers, and Sony and have won prestigious competitions such as the Austin Film Festival Screenplay Competition and the Nicholl Fellowship. See her website at *www.onthepage.tv*

$24.95 · 280 PAGES · ORDER NUMBER 149RLS · ISBN 13: 9781932907803

SAVE THE CAT!™ GOES TO THE MOVIES
THE SCREENWRITER'S GUIDE
TO EVERY STORY EVER TOLD

BLAKE SNYDER

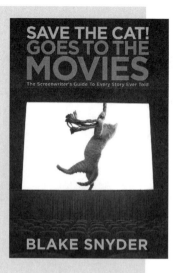

In the long-awaited sequel to his surprise bestseller, *Save the Cat!*, author and screenwriter Blake Snyder returns to form in a fast-paced follow-up that proves why his is the most talked-about approach to screenwriting in years. In the perfect companion piece to his first book, Snyder delivers even more insider's information gleaned from a 20-year track record as "one of Hollywood's most successful spec screenwriters," giving you the clues to write *your* movie.

Designed for screenwriters, novelists, and movie fans, this book gives readers the key breakdowns of the 50 most instructional movies from the past 30 years. From *M*A*S*H* to *Crash*, from *Alien* to *Saw*, from *10* to *Eternal Sunshine of the Spotless Mind*, Snyder reveals how screenwriters who came before you tackled the same challenges you are facing with the film you want to write — or the one you are currently working on.

Writing a "rom-com"? Check out the "Buddy Love" chapter for a "beat for beat" dissection of *When Harry Met Sally...* plus references to 10 other great romantic comedies that will make your story sing.

Want to execute a great mystery? Go to the "Whydunit" section and learn about the "dark turn" that's essential to the heroes of *All the President's Men*, *Blade Runner*, *Fargo* and hip noir *Brick* — and see why ALL good stories, whether a Hollywood blockbuster or a Sundance award winner, follow the same rules of structure outlined in Snyder's breakthrough method.

If you want to sell your script and create a movie that pleases most audiences most of the time, the odds increase if you reference Snyder's checklists and see what makes 50 films tick. After all, both executives and audiences respond to the same elements good writers seek to master. They want to know the type of story they signed on for, and whether it's structured in a way that satisfies everyone. It's what they're looking for. And now, it's what you can deliver.

BLAKE SNYDER, besides selling million-dollar scripts to both Disney and Spielberg, was one of Hollywood's most successful spec screenwriters. Blake's vision continues on *www.blakesnyder.com*.

$24.95 · 270 PAGES · ORDER NUMBER 75RLS · ISBN: 9781932907353

SAVE THE CAT!®
THE LAST BOOK ON SCREENWRITING YOU'LL EVER NEED!

BLAKE SNYDER

BEST SELLER

SAVE THE CAT!
The Last Book On Screenwriting You'll Ever Need!

BLAKE SNYDER

He's made millions of dollars selling screenplays to Hollywood and now screenwriter Blake Snyder tells all. "Save the Cat!®" is just one of Snyder's many ironclad rules for making your ideas more marketable and your script more satisfying — and saleable, including:
- The four elements of every winning logline.
- The seven immutable laws of screenplay physics.
- The 10 genres and why they're important to your movie.
- Why your Hero must serve your idea.
- Mastering the Beats.
- Mastering the Board to create the Perfect Beast.
- How to get back on track with ironclad and proven rules for script repair.

This ultimate insider's guide reveals the secrets that none dare admit, told by a show biz veteran who's proven that you can sell your script if you can save the cat.

"Imagine what would happen in a town where more writers approached screenwriting the way Blake suggests? My weekend read would dramatically improve, both in sellable/producible content and in discovering new writers who understand the craft of storytelling and can be hired on assignment for ideas we already have in house."
> – From the Foreword by Sheila Hanahan Taylor, Vice President, Development at Zide/Perry Entertainment, whose films include *American Pie, Cats and Dogs, Final Destination*

"One of the most comprehensive and insightful how-to's out there. Save the Cat!® *is a must-read for both the novice and the professional screenwriter."*
> – Todd Black, Producer, *The Pursuit of Happyness, The Weather Man, S.W.A.T, Alex and Emma, Antwone Fisher*

"Want to know how to be a successful writer in Hollywood? The answers are here. Blake Snyder has written an insider's book that's informative — and funny, too."
> – David Hoberman, Producer, *The Shaggy Dog* (2005), *Raising Helen, Walking Tall, Bringing Down the House, Monk* (TV)

BLAKE SNYDER, besides selling million-dollar scripts to both Disney and Spielberg, was one of Hollywood's most successful spec screenwriters. Blake's vision continues on *www.blakesnyder.com*.

$19.95 · 216 PAGES · ORDER NUMBER 34RLS · ISBN: 9781932907001

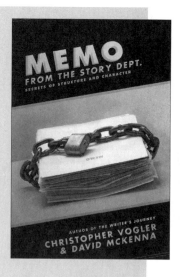

THE WRITER'S JOURNEY – 3RD EDITION
MYTHIC STRUCTURE FOR WRITERS

CHRISTOPHER VOGLER

BEST SELLER

See why this book has become an international best seller and a true classic. *The Writer's Journey* explores the powerful relationship between mythology and storytelling in a clear, concise style that's made it required reading for movie executives, screenwriters, playwrights, scholars, and fans of pop culture all over the world.

Both fiction and nonfiction writers will discover a set of useful myth-inspired storytelling paradigms (i.e., "The Hero's Journey") and step-by-step guidelines to plot and character development. Based on the work of Joseph Campbell, *The Writer's Journey* is a must for all writers interested in further developing their craft.

The updated and revised third edition provides new insights and observations from Vogler's ongoing work on mythology's influence on stories, movies, and man himself.

"This book is like having the smartest person in the story meeting come home with you and whisper what to do in your ear as you write a screenplay. Insight for insight, step for step, Chris Vogler takes us through the process of connecting theme to story and making a script come alive."
> – Lynda Obst, Producer, *Sleepless in Seattle, How to Lose a Guy in 10 Days*;
> Author, *Hello, He Lied*

"This is a book about the stories we write, and perhaps more importantly, the stories we live. It is the most influential work I have yet encountered on the art, nature, and the very purpose of storytelling."
> – Bruce Joel Rubin, Screenwriter, *Stuart Little 2, Deep Impact,*
> *Ghost, Jacob's Ladder*

CHRISTOPHER VOGLER is a veteran story consultant for major Hollywood film companies and a respected teacher of filmmakers and writers around the globe. He has influenced the stories of movies from *The Lion King* to *Fight Club* to *The Thin Red Line* and most recently wrote the first installment of *Ravenskull*, a Japanese-style manga or graphic novel. He is the executive producer of the feature film *P.S. Your Cat is Dead* and writer of the animated feature *Jester Till*.

$26.95 · 448 PAGES · ORDER NUMBER 76RLS · ISBN: 9781932907360

SELLING YOUR STORY IN 60 SECONDS
THE GUARANTEED WAY TO GET
YOUR SCREENPLAY OR NOVEL READ

MICHAEL HAUGE

BEST SELLER

Best-selling author Michael Hauge reveals:
- · How to Design, Practice, and Present the 60-Second Pitch
- · The Cardinal Rule of Pitching
- · The 10 Key Components of a Commercial Story
- · The 8 Steps to a Powerful Pitch
- · Targeting Your Buyers
- · Securing Opportunities to Pitch
- · Pitching Templates
- · And much more, including "The Best Pitch I Ever Heard," an exclusive collection from major film executives

"Michael Hauge's principles and methods are so well argued that the mysteries of effective screenwriting can be understood — even by directors."

    — Phillip Noyce, Director, *Patriot Games, Clear and Present Danger, The Quiet American, Rabbit-Proof Fence*

"... one of the few authentically good teachers out there. Every time I revisit my notes, I learn something new or reinforce something that I need to remember."

    — Jeff Arch, Screenwriter, *Sleepless in Seattle, Iron Will*

"Michael Hauge's method is magic — but unlike most magicians, he shows you how the trick is done."

    — William Link, Screenwriter & Co-Creator, *Columbo; Murder, She Wrote*

"By following the formula we learned in Michael Hauge's seminar, we got an agent, optioned our script, and now have a three-picture deal at Disney."

    — Paul Hoppe and David Henry, Screenwriters

MICHAEL HAUGE is the author of *Writing Screenplays That Sell*, now in its 30th printing, and has presented his seminars and lectures to more than 30,000 writers and filmmakers. He has coached hundreds of screenwriters and producers on their screenplays and pitches, and has consulted on projects for Warner Brothers, Disney, New Line, CBS, Lifetime, Julia Roberts, Jennifer Lopez, Kirsten Dunst, and Morgan Freeman.

$12.95 · 150 PAGES · ORDER NUMBER 64RLS · ISBN: 9781932907209

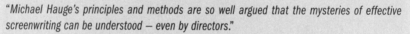

24 HOURS | **1.800.833.5738** | **WWW.MWP.COM**

CINEMATIC STORYTELLING
THE 100 MOST POWERFUL FILM CONVENTIONS
EVERY FILMMAKER MUST KNOW

JENNIFER VAN SIJLL

BEST SELLER

How do directors use screen direction to suggest conflict? How do screenwriters exploit film space to show change? How does editing style determine emotional response?

Many first-time writers and directors do not ask these questions. They forego the huge creative resource of the film medium, defaulting to dialog to tell their screen story. Yet most movies are carried by sound and picture. The industry's most successful writers and directors have mastered the cinematic conventions specific to the medium. They have harnessed non-dialog techniques to create some of the most cinematic moments in movie history.

This book is intended to help writers and directors more fully exploit the medium's inherent storytelling devices. It contains 100 non-dialog techniques that have been used by the industry's top writers and directors. From *Metropolis* and *Citizen Kane* to *Dead Man* and *Kill Bill*, the book illustrates — through 500 frame grabs and 75 script excerpts — how the inherent storytelling devices specific to film were exploited.

You will learn:
· How non-dialog film techniques can advance story.
· How master screenwriters exploit cinematic conventions to create powerful scenarios.

"*Cinematic Storytelling scores a direct hit in terms of concise information and perfectly chosen visuals, and it also searches out... and finds... an emotional core that many books of this nature either miss or are afraid of.*"
— Kirsten Sheridan, Director, *Disco Pigs*; Co-writer, *In America*

"*Here is a uniquely fresh, accessible, and truly original contribution to the field. Jennifer van Sijll takes her readers in a wholly new direction, integrating aspects of screenwriting with all the film crafts in a way I've never before seen. It is essential reading not only for screenwriters but also for filmmakers of every stripe.*"
— Prof. Richard Walter, UCLA Screenwriting Chairman

JENNIFER VAN SIJLL has taught film production, film history, and screenwriting. She is currently on the faculty at San Francisco State's Department of Cinema.

$24.95 · 230 PAGES · ORDER NUMBER 35RLS · ISBN: 9781932907056

24 HOURS | **1.800.833.5738** | WWW.MWP.COM